Power Play

Individuals in Conflict

Literary Selections for Students of English

Brenda Dyer

Acquisitions editor: Nancy Baxer
Editor: Sheryl Olinsky
Development Editor: Lida Baker
Director of production and manufacturing: Aliza Greenblatt
Editorial production/design manager: Dominick Mosco
Editorial/production supervision
  and interior design: Carey Davies, Jan Sivertsen, Merle Krumper
Production assistant: Jennifer Rella
Production Coordinator: Ray Keating
Copyeditor: Sylvia Moore, Janet Johnston

Art Director: Merle Krumper
Cover Design: Yes Graphics
Electronic Art Production: Marita Froimson, Don Kilcoyne, Carey Davies
Photo Research: Sheryl Olinsky, Jan Siversten, Nancy Baxer

PRENTICE HALL REGENTS
A VIACOM COMPANY

© 1996 by Prentice Hall Regents.
Prentice-Hall, Inc.
A Simon & Schuster Company
Upper Saddle River, New Jersey 07458

Printed in the United States of America

10   9   8   7   6   5

ISBN   0-13-122046-2

Prentice-Hall International (UK) Limited, London
Prentice-Hall of Australia Pty. Limited, Sydney
Prentice-Hall Canada Inc., Toronto
Prentice-Hall Hispanoamericana, S.A., Mexico
Prentice-Hall of India Private Limited, New Delhi
Prentice-Hall of Japan, Inc., Tokyo
Simon & Schuster Asia Pte. Ltd., Singapore
Editora Prentice-Hall do Brasil, Ltda., Rio de Janeiro

Contents

POWER PLAY TEXT PERMISSIONS LIST

Acknowledgments

The author wishes to express her gratitude to the authors who agreed to have their work included in *Power Play*, and especially author Paul Milenski for his kind, lively interest in the text. Thanks also to Robert Scholes for the inspiration for the Introduction.

Special thanks to ESL editor Nancy Baxer of Prentice Hall Regents for her loyal, enthusiastic support, production editors Carey Davies and Jan Sivertsen, and permissions editor Sheryl Olinsky, who worked so meticulously.

I am also grateful to Susan Johnston, former director of the Intensive English Language Program at Temple University, Tokyo, for her encouragement at the early stages of the book, to my students at Temple, who read and discussed the stories with me, and to the instructors of the English Language Program at International Christian University, Tokyo, who kindly class-tested some of the stories.

As always, I appreciate the sage advice and encouragement of Barbara and Frank Dyer.

Photograph Credits

Cover: Merle Krumper (bottom right); USDA (bottom left); National Archives (middle left); VISTA (middle right); Ken Karp (background). **Unit One:** VISTA (p. 6); Sheryl Olinsky (pp. 8-11). **Unit Two:** Plymouth Plantation (bottom pp. 20, 22-23); Nancy Baxer (top left pp. 60-67); Charles Gatewood (top right pp. 20, 23); Teri Leigh Stratford (p. 28); Sheryl Olinsky (pp. 30-33); Stephen Capra (pp. 36, 38-51); Laimute E. Druskis (pp. 38-51); Eugene Gordon (pp. 38-51); United Nations/M. Grant (p. 58); Franklin D. Roosevelt Library (bottom right pp. 60-67); Merle Krumper (pp. 72); Ken Karp (top right pp. 60-67); San Francisco Convention & Visitors Bureau (pp. 38-51); Library of Congress (pp. 19, 38-51); Consumer Relations Department (bottom left pp. 60-67); National Archives, Standard Oil Co. (NJ). **Unit Three:** Resorts International Hotel Casino (p. 82, 84-85); Nancy Baxer (pp. 92-95); Laimute E. Druskus (p. 90); Ken Karp (pp. 81, 100); E. Mandelmann (p. 114); USDA Photo (p. 126); Marc Anderson (pp. 102, 106); Irene Springer (pp. 103, 108); Teri Leigh Stratford (pp. 104,109); The Hoover Co. North Canton, Ohio (p. 124); New York Convention & Visitors Bureau (pp. 104-105, 107). **Unit Four:** Merle Krumper (pp. 136-141); Marc Anderson (pp. 144-149); New York Convention & Visitors Bureau (p. 134); Ken Karp (pp. 154, 161); Anita Duncan (pp. 159,164); U.S. Forest Service (pp. 157, 160, 166); Standard Oil Co. (NJ) (middle right and far left pp. 133, 152, 156, 158, 162, 163, 165); Irene Springer (pp. 155, 167); Laimute Druskis (far right pp. 133, 177); Meryl Joseph (p. 176); National Archives (middle left pp. 133, 178); Library of Congress (pp. 179-180); AT&T Co. Photo Center (p. 182); Baush & Lomb (p. 182 dots). **Unit Five:** USDA (pp. 187-188); Vermont Travel Division (pp. 191, 193, 195, 197, 199, 201, 203, 205, 207, 209, 211); Tennessee Valley Authority (pp. 192, 194, 196, 198, 200, 202, 204, 206, 208, 210, 212).

Also Desk Art by Zedcor vol 2.0 for Unit Three (pp. 116-119, background 114-115).

UNIT 1

INTRODUCTION

▲▲▲▲▲

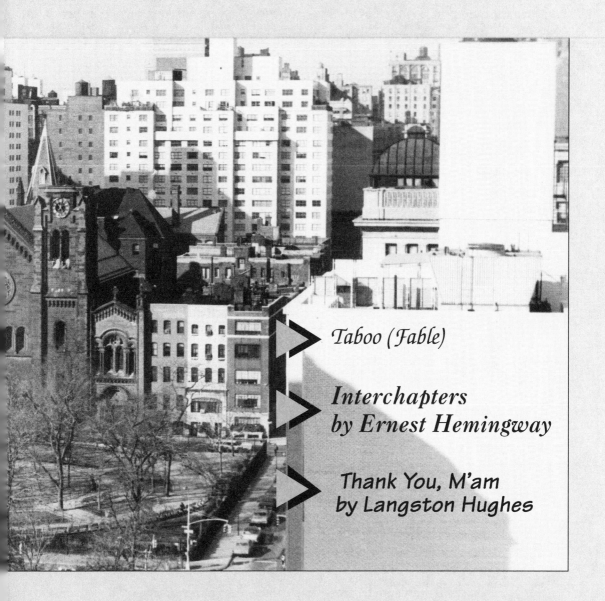

Why Read a Story?

This collection of North American stories, poems, and a play is prepared for students of English. It is said that "conflict is the soul of fiction." The unifying theme of this collection is "power" as it expressed in the external and internal conflicts which fuel individual, interpersonal, and social interactions.

Why read a story? Eighteenth century British essayist Samuel Johnson said writers write stories "to instruct and to entertain"; therefore we may read stories to be instructed and entertained. But why read a story as students of English? You will be instructed in ways Johnson probably did not intend:

- enriching your vocabulary
- developing reading skills such as guessing vocabulary from context, skimming, scanning, inferring, and interpreting
- practicing listening and speaking skills in informal and formal classroom discussions and presentations
- developing your writing skills as you respond in journals and essays to the stories

You will add to your "literary competence": knowledge of traditional Western literary conventions and use of such things as irony, metaphor, and symbolism, which will prepare you for further study of literature. You will add to your understanding of North American culture, and in the process of comparison and evaluation, of your own. And, as Johnson suggested, you will be both instructed by the truth of fiction in the ways of the human heart and entertained by the follies and ironies of our human condition.

What Is a Story?

What are the differences between a newspaper article and fiction? Between part of a narrative and a "story"? What is a story?

Read the following passages. The teacher will assign one passage to each group. In your group, decide:

- Is this passage a story?
- If you say it is, what elements does it have that make it a story?
- If you decide it is not a story, what elements of a story does it lack?

Be prepared to explain your decision to the class.

Taboo

His guardian angel whispered to Fabian, behind his shoulder: "Careful Fabian! It is decreed that you will die the minute you pronounce the word 'doyen.'"

"Doyen?" asked Fabian, intrigued.

And he died.

Interchapter

While the bombardment was knocking the trench to pieces at Fossalta, he lay very flat and sweated and prayed oh Jesus Christ get me out of here. Dear Jesus please get me out. Christ please please please Christ. If you'll only keep me from getting killed I'll do anything you say. I believe in you and I'll tell everyone in the world that you are the only one that matters. Please please please dear Jesus. The shelling moved further up the line. We went to work on the trench and in the morning the sun came up and the day was hot and muggy and cheerful and quiet. The next night back at Mestre he did not tell the girl he went upstairs with at the Villa Rossa about Jesus. And he never told anybody.

Interchapter

We were in a garden at Mons. Young Buckley came in with his patrol from across the river. The first German I saw climbed up over the garden wall. We waited till he got one leg over and then potted him. He had so much equipment on and looked awfully surprised and fell down into the garden. Then three more came over further down the wall. We shot them. They all came just like that.

How to Read a Story

A. ELEMENTS OF FICTION

In your discussion, you probably identified the following elements of a story:

setting   character   plot   conflict   point of view   theme

Looking for details about each of these elements will help you understand how the author created his or her story.

B. SOME READING STRATEGIES

1. Read with purpose.

The reading skills that you will develop in your study of these stories will help you in further reading for pleasure or academic study.

Form questions as you read and look for the answers. It may guide your understanding if you keep the following general questions in mind as you read:

⮕ *Who* are the main characters? What do you know about them?

⮕ *Where* does the story take place?

⮕ *When* does the story take place?

⮕ *What* happens?

⮕ *What* **changes** occur in the story?

2. Don't read too slowly.

Reading "word-by-word" usually means that you are translating, which does not help your comprehension or concentration. In your first reading of the story, it is helpful to:

⮕ **Read the story quickly** once without a dictionary or glossary.

⮕ **Accept the anxiety** of not understanding everything. Do not worry if you cannot understand details or if you come across many difficult words.

⮕ **Make predictions and form questions** with your limited understanding. You will answer these in your second or third readings.

3. Study vocabulary selectively.

You don't need to understand *every* word.

To demonstrate how much meaning you can make out of a literary text without knowing all the words, read the following first paragraph of a story and answer the True or False questions which follow it.

She was a _____ woman with a _____ purse that had everything in it but a hammer and nails. It had a long strap and she _____ it slung across her shoulder. It was about _____ at night, dark, and she was walking _____, when a boy ran up behind her and tried to _____ her purse. The strap broke with the sudden single _____ the boy gave it from behind. But the boy's weight and the weight of the _____ combined caused him to lose his _____. Instead of taking off _____ as he had hoped, the boy _____ on his back on the sidewalk and his legs _____ up. The large woman simply turned around and _____ him right square in his blue-jeaned sitter. Then she reached down, _____ the boy up by his shirt front, and __ him until his teeth _____.

True or False?

_____ 1. This story takes place in the morning.
_____ 2. The woman was small and weak.
_____ 3. She carried a large purse.
_____ 4. She was probably a rich woman.
_____ 5. A small boy tried to steal her purse.
_____ 6. He didn't succeed.

What you have done is similar to reading a paragraph of 200 words, not knowing the meaning of one or two words per line. The skill of guessing from context can be developed, and it is the one vocabulary objective for this course.

Expect to read a story more than once, each time with a different purpose. The second vocabulary objective is increasing your active and passive vocabulary. It is not the best use of your time to translate these stories; the time students take looking up words in the dictionary is not necessary time spent improving their English!

- **Guess** from context.
- **Use a dictionary only when necessary;** learn to accept a certain degree of uncertainty.
- **Use the glossary,** the questions and exercises, and class discussion to make meaning of the text.
- Spend your preparation and study time, **not in translation,** but in studying the glossary, seeing how the glossed words work in the context of the story, and so adding to your vocabulary.
- **Keep a vocabulary journal.**

Thank You, M'am

by Langston Hughes

"You ought to be my son. I would teach you right from wrong. Least I can do right now is to wash your face. Are you hungry?"

GUIDING QUESTIONS

Read the story once quickly without using your dictionary. It is not necessary that you understand every word. Just concentrate on getting the main ideas.

1. **Who** are the main characters? What do you know about them?

2. **Where** does the story take place?

3. **When** does the story take place?

4. **What** happens?

5. **What changes** occur in the story?

SHE WAS A LARGE WOMAN with a large purse that had everything in it but a hammer and nails. It had a long strap, and she carried it slung across her shoulder. It was about eleven o'clock at night, dark, and she was walking alone, when a boy ran

5 up behind her and tried to snatch her purse. The strap broke with the sudden single tug the boy gave it from behind. But the boy's weight and the weight of the purse combined caused him to lose his balance. Instead of taking off full blast as he had hoped, the boy fell on his back on the sidewalk and his legs flew up. The

10 large woman simply turned around and kicked him right square in his blue-jeaned sitter. Then she reached down, picked the boy up by his shirt front, and shook him until his teeth rattled.

After that the woman said, "Pick up my pocketbook, boy, and give it here."

15 She still held him tightly. But she bent down enough to permit him to stoop and pick up her purse. Then she said, "Now ain't you ashamed of yourself?"

Firmly gripped by his shirt front, the boy said, "Yes'm."

The woman said, "What did you want to do it for?"

20 The boy said, "I didn't aim to."

She said, "You a lie!"

By that time two or three people passed, stopped, turned to look, and some stood watching.

"If I turn you loose, will you run?" asked the woman.

25 "Yes'm," said the boy.

"Then I won't turn you loose," said the woman. She did not release him.

"Lady, I'm sorry," whispered the boy.

"Um-hum! Your face is dirty. I got a great mind to wash your

30 face for you. Ain't you got nobody home to tell you to wash your face?"

"No'm," said the boy.

"Then it will get washed this evening," said the large woman, starting up the street, dragging the frightened boy behind her.

35 He looked as if he were fourteen or fifteen, frail and willow-wild, in tennis shoes and blue jeans.

The woman said, "You ought to be my son. I would teach you right from wrong. Least I can do right now is to wash your face. Are you hungry?"

40 "No'm," said the being-dragged boy. "I just want you to turn me loose."

"Was I bothering *you* when I turned that corner?" asked the woman.

"No'm."

45 "But you put yourself in contact with *me*," said the woman. "If you think that that contact is not going to last awhile, you got another thought coming. When I get through with you, sir, you are going to remember Mrs. Luella Bates Washington Jones."

Sweat popped out on the boy's face and he began to struggle.
50 Mrs. Jones stopped, jerked him around in front of her, put a half nelson about his neck, and continued to drag him up the street. When she got to her door, she dragged the boy inside, down a hall, and into a large kitchenette-furnished room at the rear of the house. She switched on the light and left the door open. The boy
55 could hear other roomers laughing and talking in the large house. Some of their doors were open, too, so he knew he and the woman were not alone. The woman still had him by the neck in the middle of her room.

She said, "What is your name?"

60 "Roger," answered the boy.

"Then, Roger, you go to that sink and wash your face," said the woman, whereupon she turned him loose—at last. Roger looked at the door—looked at the woman—looked at the door—*and went to the sink.*

65 "Let the water run until it gets warm," she said. "Here's a clean towel."

"You gonna take me to jail?" asked the boy, bending over

the sink.

"Not with that face, I would not take you nowhere," said the
woman. "Here I am trying to get home to cook me a bite to eat,
and you snatch my pocketbook! Maybe you ain't been to your
supper either, late as it be. Have you?"

"There's nobody home at my house," said the boy.

"Then we'll eat," said the woman. "I believe you're hungry—or
been hungry—to try to snatch my pocketbook!"

"I want a pair of blue suede shoes," said the boy.

"Well, you didn't have to snatch *my* pocketbook to get some
suede shoes," said Mrs. Luella Bates Washington Jones. "You
could of asked me."

"M'am?"

The water dripping from his face, the boy looked at her. There
was a long pause. A very long pause. After he had dried his face,
and not knowing what else to do, dried it again, the boy turned
around, wondering what next. The door was open. He could
make a dash for it down the hall. He could run, run, run, *run*!

The woman was sitting on the daybed. After a while she said,
"I were young once and I wanted things I could not get."

There was another long pause. The boy's mouth opened. Then
he frowned, not knowing he frowned.

The woman said, "Um-hum! You thought I was going to say
but, didn't you? You thought I was going to say, *but I didn't snatch
people's pocketbooks.* Well, I wasn't going to say that." Pause.
Silence. "I have done things, too, which I would not tell you, son—
neither tell God, if He didn't already know. Everybody's got
something in common. So you set down while I fix us something
to eat. You might run that comb through your hair so you will
look presentable."

In another corner of the room behind a screen was a gas plate
and an icebox. Mrs. Jones got up and went behind the screen.
The woman did not watch the boy to see if he was going to run
now, nor did she watch her purse, which she left behind her on

the daybed. But the boy took care to sit on the far side of the room, away from the purse, where he thought she could easily see him out of the corner of her eye if she wanted to. He did not trust the woman *not* to trust him. And he did not want to be mistrusted now.

"Do you need somebody to go to the store," asked the boy, "maybe to get some milk or something?"

"Don't believe I do," said the woman, "unless you just want sweet milk yourself. I was going to make cocoa out of this canned milk I got here."

"That will be fine," said the boy.

She heated some lima beans and ham she had in the icebox, made the cocoa, and set the table. The woman did not ask the boy anything about where he lived, or his folks, or anything else that would embarrass him. Instead, as they ate, she told him about her job in a hotel beauty shop that stayed open late, what the work was like, and how all kinds of women came in and out, blonds, redheads, and Spanish. Then she cut him a half of her ten-cent cake.

"Eat some more, son," she said.

When they were finished eating, she got up and said, "Now here, take this ten dollars and buy yourself some blue suede shoes. And next time, do not make the mistake of latching onto *my* pocketbook *nor nobody else's*—because shoes got by devilish ways will burn your feet. I got to get my rest now. But from here on in, son, I hope you will behave yourself."

She led him down the hall to the front door and opened it. "Good night! Behave yourself, boy!" she said, looking out into the street as he went down the steps.

The boy wanted to say something other than, "Thank you, M'am," to Mrs. Luella Bates Washington Jones, but although his lips moved, he couldn't even say that as he turned at the foot of the barren stoop and looked up at the large woman in the door. Then she shut the door.

Thank You, M'am

Glossary

to sling	to put or throw across (past participle is "slung")
to snatch	to take quickly
a tug	a small pull
full blast (idiom)	as quickly as possible, with all one's energy
"sitter" (slang)	buttocks
to rattle	to make a dry, sharp sound, especially by shaking
to stoop	to bend over
"ain't"	slang for "are not"
to grip	to hold tightly
to aim	to have a purpose
"turn you loose" (idiom)	let you go
frail	weak, small
"you've got another thought coming" (idiom)	you're wrong, you'll soon change your mind
to put a nelson (idiom)	to use a wrestling hold in which you put your arm under your opponent's arm and push your hand against his neck
"a bite to eat" (idiom)	a small lunch or snack
to pause	to stop doing something for a minute
"to make a dash for it" (idiom)	to try to escape
to frown	to make a puzzled or angry face
presentable	good enough to show
to latch onto	to hold tightly
"by devilish ways" (idiom)	by a bad or unethical way
barren	empty, sterile
a stoop	porch or stairs at the entrance of a house

SECOND READING

After you have read the story once without the glossary or dictionary, re-read it with the glossary. Then answer the following True or False questions:

Comprehension Check

True or False?

_____ 1. Mrs. Jones is a coward.

_____ 2. She dragged Roger into her apartment.

_____ 3. He was about 8 years old.

_____ 4. Mrs. Jones owned a large house.

_____ 5. The boy tried to snatch her purse in order to get money for food.

_____ 6. Mrs. Jones admitted that she had done bad things too when she was young.

_____ 7. Her "kitchen" is just the corner of one big room.

_____ 8. She works in a beauty shop.

_____ 9. Roger hides the 10 dollars which he stole from her.

Comprehension Check: Plot Summary

Write a plot summary of about 100 words with the following key words:

    Mrs. Jones   Roger   steal   supper   blue suede shoes   10 dollars   thank you

Try to use some of the following connectors in your summary:

    furthermore / however / on the other hand / to make matters worse / finally

Interpretation

Use the following "Guide for Reading Short Stories" to analyze the story's elements of setting, plot, characters, conflict, climax, symbol, point of view, tone, irony and theme.

A Guide for Reading Short Stories

Story Title   Thank You, M'am by *Langston Hughes*

Setting   *The place and time* in which a story takes place.

Plot   What happens in the story.

Characters   Describing a character means describing his or her background, motivation, and personality. Character is revealed by (1) what the author says about him or her; (2) what the character says and does; and (3) how other characters react to him or her. Often a short story shows some kind of change in the main character's situation, attitude, or understanding.

Conflict   The struggle between characters, between a character and an outside circumstance, or even between two choices within the same character. Plot depends on conflict.

Climax   The "turning point" of highest tension in the story. A change usually occurs at the climax in which the character's conflict is resolved.

Symbol	An object or act in the story that seems to represent a deeper or larger meaning, usually one connected with the theme.
Point of view	Who tells the story. "*Omniscient* point of view" means a narrator who knows everything about the characters and stands outside the story. "*Limited* third person point of view" means that the story is narrated by someone who stands outside the story but who sees everything from the viewpoint of only one character. "*First person* point of view" means that the writer lets one of the characters tell the story as "I."
Tone	The emotional feeling conveyed by the author to the reader (serious, light, humorous, ironic, grim, etc.).
Irony	A difference between what is expected and what happens. Irony may occur in a surprise ending, or when the character's understanding of the story situation is different from the reader's knowledge.
Theme	The main idea illustrated by the story; the main insight which the story gives us about human life.

Which of these elements of fiction do you think is most important in *this* story?

Evaluation: Discussion or Response Journal

1. When you were a child, was there something like "blue suede shoes" that you longed for? Why do you suppose Roger wanted the blue suede shoes so badly? What might they symbolize? (Note: a symbol is a thing, person, action, or event that stands for something else (for example, night = death).
2. Can you compare or contrast Roger's experience to any experience of your own?
3. Do Roger or Mrs. Jones remind you of anyone you know? Describe that person.
4. Why did Mrs. Jones give him the money? What do you think about her treatment of Roger?
5. Imagine another response Mrs. Jones might have had to Roger (for example, she might have taken him to the police). How would the story change?

Writing Assignment

Read the following paragraph which describes the character of Roger:

> Roger, one of the main characters in the story, *Thank You, M'am* by Langston Hughes, has a distrustful nature which is challenged by the trust and wholehearted generosity of Mrs. Jones. He does not expect anyone to be kind to him; he is used to trying aggressively to get what he needs or wants, even if it means stealing the money from a poor old woman. He waits for Mrs. Jones to take him to jail, but instead she offers him food, money, advice, and love. The young thief, puzzled by her response, keeps watching the door of her room, planning to run, and even asks her if he can go to the store to buy her some milk in the hope of escape. In the end, he is forced to accept her generosity and he struggles to find the proper words to repay Mrs. Jones. Though he is speechless, we sense that he is thankful and impressed by her loving action, as he hesitates at her front door before she says goodbye.

In the paragraph above, underline the sentence in which the main topic is expressed. Number each supporting example of Roger's "distrustful" nature. What is the purpose of the two concluding sentences?

Now write a paragraph which describes the character of Mrs. Jones. Don't forget a topic sentence, two or three supporting examples, and a concluding sentence.

Vocabulary Analysis

Keep a vocabulary journal (perhaps at the back of your Response Journal) in which you keep a list like this one for each story you read.

Story Title   Thank You, M'am by *Langston Hughes*

For each new word, locate the source, copy the sentence from the story, write a definition, and make up your own sentence which illustrates the meaning of the new word.

Word	to aim
Parts of speech	aim (n), aim (v), aimless (adj)
Source: *p. 8, l. 20*	Definition: *to intend, to have a purpose*
Story sentence:	*The boy said, "I didn't aim to."*
My sentence:	*I aim to graduate next spring.*

1. Word: _____   Parts of Speech: _____

   Source: _____   Definition: _____

   _____

   Story Sentence: _____

   _____

   My Sentence: _____

   _____

UNIT 2

FAMILY TIES

▲▲▲▲▲

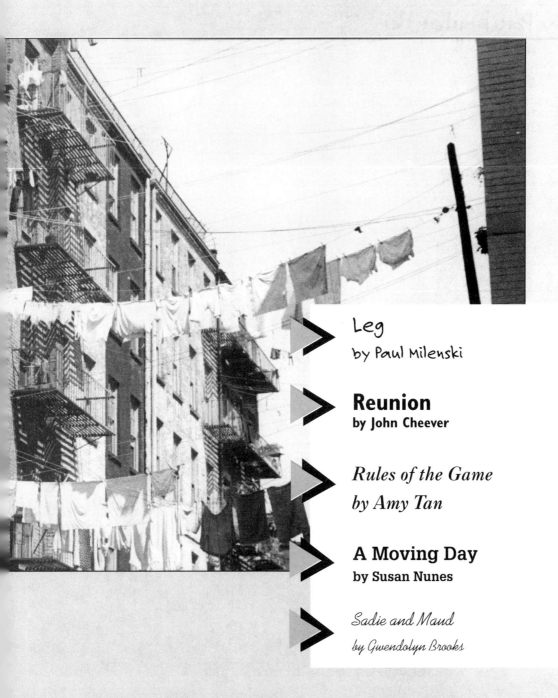

Leg

by Paul Milenski

"He ought to ignore it, he told himself,
it was such a little thing."

Background:

Sometimes a story takes place almost entirely in a character's mind. In this short-short story, we experience Frank's indecision as he moves back and forth from "should I stay?" to "should I go?" in both the past and the present.

Warm-up Discussion/Response Journal:

When you are 20 years old, what are some important decisions you have to make? 30 years old? 45 years old? Can you think of any decisions that might hurt other people?

Guiding Questions:

Read the story once quickly. It is not necessary that you understand every word. Just concentrate on getting the main ideas.

1. *Who* are the main characters? What do you know about them?
2. *Where* does the story take place?
3. *When* does the story take place?
4. *What* happens?
5. *What changes* occur in the story?

LOOKING OUT HIS LIVING ROOM WINDOW

Frank saw a brown object fluttering on the stockade fence
that separated his yard from the neighbor's. The fluttering
was near the top of the fence where the flat laths took the
shape of rounded arrowheads. Frank assumed the object was
5   a leaf blown down by the Autumn breeze; it rested when
the wind died, fluttered when it blew again.

    But then lately Frank had been seeing things. He had quit
smoking, was straining terribly to control his habit. His
10   daughter had encouraged him to do so. "Daddy, it's so bad
for you. It gives you heart attacks and cancer. Please don't
smoke." So with his daughter living apart from him at her
mother's, Frank quit as appeasement to his little child. But
there was this side effect to his abstinence: what he gained
15   in peripheral vision from the smoke cloud lifted from his
retinae, he lost in clarity (no, it was not clarity)—he lost in
definition among the many more objects he now as non-
smoker could see.

    To keep his hands busy, he went into the kitchen, did the
20   crossword in the daily paper, made himself a snack, washed
the dishes. Then he went into the bedroom, put his clothes
away, made the bed, was passing through the living room to
get the vacuum cleaner when he looked out the window
again. There was the fluttering, more compelling, almost
25   urgent. He pressed his face to the window, realized a new
condition: the wind had died down; there was not a stir of
leaves or branches. He ought to ignore it, he told himself, it
was such a little thing. But after he readjusted his daughter's
photograph on the end table, he opened the door, stepped
30   outside. But even closer to the object, his vision
unobstructed, he could still not make out what it was. He
was going to turn, go back inside, but there was something

imperative about the fluttering, something that *made* him move forward.

35   He walked toward the fence, his eyes fixed on the object, but here a ray of sunshine gleamed, caught him with its brightness. He closed his eyes, saw a vision from his past. He was in the kitchen of his old house, with his ex-wife (then wife), his daughter, a tad younger, as faithfully filial as

40 now—daddy's girl. But she was under the kitchen table, her legs pulled to her chest, sobbing uncontrollably. He was holding packed bags, his ex-wife pointing demonstrably to the door. "Get out, Frank!" But then his daughter reached out from under the table, grasped her daddy's leg. "No,

45 daddy. Please don't go. Please, daddy." He felt his little daughter's soft hands against his leg.

    He was halfway across the lawn when he noticed the object was not a leaf. It was fuller, rounder, did not have the shape or thinness of a leaf. It was a little bird, and at

50 the fence he saw it was a sparrow, its breast mottled brown, its throat white, bright yellow slashes above its eyes. Its spindly thinnish leg was caught between laths, pinched and held there, so the sparrow could only spin around, flutter, as on a short tether. Its leg was twisted, turned round and

55 round from its fluttering, like a thin copper wire when turned and bent repeatedly. The leg was bleeding, thin watery drops of blood.

    Frank reached the bird, wanted to hold it, to break the laths away. But the bird fluttered, spun away from him; then

60 to escape from being touched by a human hand, it gave itself a violent suicidal jerk, tore itself off the fence leaving its sticklike leg behind. Oh God! Frank felt for his own leg, actually fell to the ground, pulled its thinness to his chest.

Leg

Glossary

to flutter	to wave or flap quickly and irregularly
stockade fence	a protective fence made of upright stakes
lath	a narrow strip of wood
arrowhead	the pointed tip of an arrow
to strain	to try very hard
appeasement	an action to satisfy someone who is upset
abstinence	stopping one's own action; for example, giving up smoking or drinking
peripheral vision	the area of vision just outside (at the side of) one's direct sight
retinae	the back of the eyeballs, which are sensitive to light
compelling	forceful, attractive
urgent	very important
a stir	a movement
unobstructed	free or clear of any blocks
imperative	very important
"a tad younger" (idiom)	a little younger
to grasp	to take and hold strongly
mottled	spotted
spindly	very, very thin
a tether	a rope to which an animal is tied

Comprehension Check

1. What does Frank think he sees caught in his fence?
2. Why did he need to "keep his hands busy"? How did he do so?
3. The object continued to flutter in the fence. What was strange about that?
4. Why did he close his eyes? Summarize his flashback.
5. What was wrong with the bird?
6. What finally happened to the bird? Why?
7. What happened to Frank?

Interpretation: A Closer Look at Language

1. *"But there was this side effect to his abstinence: what he gained in peripheral vision from the smoke cloud lifted from his retinae, he lost in clarity (no, it was not clarity)– he lost in definition among the many more objects he now as non-smoker could see."*

Choose the best word to complete the paraphrase below:

started, quit, hate, notice, direction, definition, leave, see, clear, confused.

> When he _____ smoking, he began to _____ everything around him much more. However, although he improved his vision, he lost his sense of _____. In other words, to be able to _____ so many more things made him feel _____ or perhaps overwhelmed.

Do you think that this description is referring only to Frank's physical eyesight?

2. *"Frank felt for his own leg, actually fell to the ground, pulled its thinness to his chest."*

What does "it" refer to? What effect does writing the sentence this way–with commas and no conjunctions–have on the reader?

3. The title of this story is "Leg." Find the references to a leg and fill in the chart below. The first one is done for you.

	Reference to "leg"	Verb used	Who?	Emotion
1.	her legs pulled to her chest	pulled	daughter	sadness, desire for security
2.				
3.				
4.				
5.				
6.				
7.				
8.				

Notice how the verbs help to create the emotional tone of the story.

Evaluation: Discussion or Response Journal

1. Why does Milenski set up the parallels between Frank, the daughter, and the bird? What is he comparing? Would you consider the bird a symbol, and if so, of what?

2. What emotional effect did this story have on you?

Reunion

by John Cheever

"He was a stranger to me – my mother divorced him three years ago, and I hadn't been with him since – but as soon as I saw him I felt that he was my father, my flesh and blood, my future and my doom."

Background:

A father and teenage son meet after being separated for three years. Cheever poignantly captures the anxiety of the expectations of that meeting.

Warm-up discussion/Response Journal:

What does the word "reunion" make you think of? Does it have a happy or sad connotation?

Sit with a partner. One of you is the father, the other the son. Imagine that you are meeting for the first time in three years. What do you say to each other? How do you feel? Role–play a short dialogue.

Listen:

Listen as your teacher reads the story aloud to you. As you listen, consider these guiding questions:

1. ***Who*** are the main characters? What do you know about them?

2. ***Where*** does the story take place?

3. ***When*** does the story take place?

4. ***What*** happens?

5. ***What changes*** occur in the story?

Comprehension: Group Summary — 50 words less – group

Sit with two or three other students. Together, create an oral summary of the story. Do not worry if you didn't catch all the details; just do your best in your group to share what you did understand, and re-create the basic plot of the story. Your teacher may ask you to choose a spokesperson for your group and share your summary with the class.

THE LAST TIME I SAW my father was in Grand Central Station. I was going from my grandmother's in the Adirondacks to a cottage on the Cape that my mother had rented, and I wrote my father that I would be in New York
5 between trains for an hour and a half and asked if we could have lunch together. His secretary wrote to say that he would meet me at the information booth at noon, and at twelve o'clock sharp I saw him coming through the crowd. He was a stranger to me–my mother divorced him three years ago,
10 and I hadn't been with him since–but as soon as I saw him I felt that he was my father, my flesh and blood, my future and my doom. I knew that when I was grown I would be something like him; I would have to plan my campaigns within his limitations. He was a big, good-looking man, and I
15 was terribly happy to see him again. He struck me on the back and shook my hand. "Hi, Charlie," he said. "Hi, boy. I'd like to take you up to my club, but it's in the Sixties, and if you have to catch an early train I guess we'd better get something to eat around here." He put his arm around me,
20 and I smelled my father the way my mother sniffs a rose. It was a rich compound of whiskey, after-shave lotion, shoe polish, woolens, and the rankness of a mature male. I hoped that someone would see us together. I wished that we could be photographed. I wanted some record of our having been
25 together.

We went out of the station and up a side street to a restaurant. It was still early, and the place was empty. The bartender was quarreling with a delivery boy, and there was one very old waiter in a red coat down by the kitchen door. We sat down, and my father hailed the waiter in a loud voice. *"Kellner!"* he

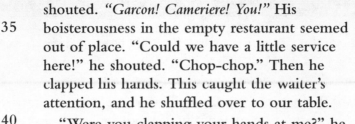

shouted. *"Garcon! Cameriere! You!"* His
boisterousness in the empty restaurant seemed
out of place. "Could we have a little service
here!" he shouted. "Chop-chop." Then he
clapped his hands. This caught the waiter's
attention, and he shuffled over to our table.

"Were you clapping your hands at me?" he
asked.

"Calm down, calm down, *sommelier*," my father said. "If it
isn't too much to ask of you–if it wouldn't be too much
above and beyond the call of duty, we would like a couple of
Beefeater Gibsons."

"I don't like to be clapped at," the waiter said.

"I should have brought my whistle," my father said. "I
have a whistle that is audible only to the ears of old waiters.
Now, take out your little pad and your little pencil and see if
you can get this straight: two Beefeater Gibsons. Repeat
after me: two Beefeater Gibsons."

"I think you'd better go somewhere else," the waiter said
quietly.

"That," said my father, "is one of the most brilliant
suggestions I have ever heard. Come on, Charlie, let's get
the hell out of here."

I followed my father out of that restaurant into another.
He was not so boisterous this time. Our drinks came, and he
cross-questioned me about the baseball season. He then
struck the edge of his empty glass with his knife and began
shouting again. *"Garcon! Kellner! You!* Could we trouble you
to bring us two more of the same."

"How old is the boy?" the waiter asked.

"That," my father said, "is none of your goddamned
business."

"I'm sorry, sir," the waiter said, "but I won't serve the boy
another drink."

"Well, I have some news for you," my father said. "I have

35

40

45

50

55

60

65

some very interesting news for you. This doesn't happen to be the only restaurant in New York. They've opened another on the corner. Come on, Charlie."

He paid the bill, and I followed him out of that restaurant into another. Here the waiters wore pink jackets like hunting coats, and there was a lot of horse tack on the walls. We sat down, and my father began to shout again. "Master of the hounds! Tallyhoo and all that sort of thing. We'd like a little something in the way of a stirrup cup. Namely, two Bibson Geefeaters."

"Two Bibson Geefeaters?" the waiter asked, smiling.

"You know damned well what I want," my father said angrily. "I want two Beefeater Gibsons, and make it snappy. Things have changed in jolly old England. So my friend the duke tells me. Let's see what England can produce in the way of a cocktail."

"This isn't England," the waiter said.

"Don't argue with me," my father said. "Just do as you're told."

"I just thought you might like to know where you are," the waiter said.

"If there is one thing I cannot tolerate," my father said, "it is an impudent domestic. Come on, Charlie."

The fourth place we went to was Italian. "*Buon giorno,*" my father said. "*Per favore, possiamo avere due cocktail americani, forti, forti. Molto gin, poco vermut.*"

"I don't understand Italian," the waiter said.

"Oh, come off it," my father said. "You understand Italian, and you know damned well you do. Vogliamo due cocktail americani. Subito."

The waiter left us and spoke with the

captain, who came over to our table and said, "I'm sorry, sir, but this table is reserved."

100   "All right," my father said. "Get us another table."

"All the tables are reserved," the captain said.

"I get it," my father said. "You don't desire our patronage. Is that it? Well, the hell with you. *Vada all' inferno*. Let's go, Charlie."

"I have to get my train," I said.

105   "I'm sorry, sonny," my father said. "I'm terribly sorry." He put his arm around me and pressed me against him. "I'll walk you back to the station. If there had only been time to go up to my club."

"That's all right, Daddy," I said.

"I'll get you a paper," he said. "I'll get you a paper to read on the
110 train."

Then he went up to a newsstand and said, "Kind sir, will you be good enough to favor me with one of your goddamned, no-good, ten-cent afternoon papers?" The clerk turned away from him and stared at a magazine cover. "Is it asking too much, kind sir," my
115 father said, "is it asking too much for you to sell me one of your disgusting specimens of yellow journalism?"

"I have to go, Daddy," I said. "It's late."

"Now, just wait a second, sonny," he said. "Just wait a second. I want to get a rise out of this chap."

120   "Goodbye, Daddy," I said, and I went down the stairs and got my train, and that was the last time I saw my father.

Reunion

Glossary

Grand Central Station	the main train station in New York City
the Adirondacks	the name of a mountain range in New York State
the Cape	Cape Cod, Massachusetts
one's flesh and blood	one's relatives
doom	a bad destiny, a bad fate
a campaign	a series of planned activities, with a set purpose (as a military campaign)
boisterous	very noisy and active
"That is none of your goddamned business" (idiom)	a rude way of saying "I won't answer your question because it does not concern you."
impudent	rude
a domestic	a servant
patronage	support given by a regular customer
"to get a rise out of someone" (idiom)	to cause someone to become upset or angry

expectations / reality

Comprehension and Interpretation

Now, read the story and answer the following questions.

1. With a partner or in groups of three, decide which of these adjectives are most and which are least appropriate to the father. For each adjective, find words or lines from the story to support your decision.

shy	boisterous	nervous
lonely	rude	vain
pedantic	impatient	caring about his son
punctual	soft-spoken	elegant
modest	bossy	sarcastic
showoff	handsome	strict

2. Do the father and son speak much to each other? Why do you suppose that is?

3. Compare the mood of the first paragraph with that of the last paragraph.

Evaluation: Discussion or Response Journal

Why does the father act the way he does?

Do you think this story is realistic? Why or why not?

What might you have done if you were this young man? Was this reunion what you expected?

Pleasant + unpleasant reunions?

Cartoon — overhead

4 own reunion Pete in England

Nova Scotia

Rules of the Game

by Amy Tan

"At the next tournament, I won again, but it was my mother who wore the triumphant grin."

Background:

"Rules of the Game," one of the first stories which Amy Tan wrote, eventually was included in her collection, *The Joy Luck Club*, which was then made into a popular film. The story describes not only the game of chess but the "games" played between mother and daughter. The story gives a sense of the universal and deeply felt power dynamics between parent and child.

Warm-up discussion:

Answer the following questionnaire (True or False) about your family's attitudes. Then compare your results with a few classmates.

1. My mother (father) often pressures me about my future plans.
2. My own dreams for school, job, marriage, etc. are quite different from my parents' expectations for me.
3. Sometimes I feel my parents are trying to live out their success through my life.
4. I have openly disagreed with my parents about their expectations for me.
5. Much of my success so far in life, I can attribute to my parents.

Listen/Response Journal:

Listen as your teacher reads aloud the first three paragraphs of the story. Explain in your own words the lesson the mother was trying to teach the little girl. Do you recall any similar lesson from your parents? Do you agree with this life "strategy"?

Guiding Questions:

Read the story once quickly. It is not necessary that you understand every word. Just concentrate on getting the main ideas.

1. *Who* are the main characters? What do you know about them?
2. *Where* does the story take place?
3. *When* does the story take place?
4. *What* happens?
5. *What Changes* occur in the story?

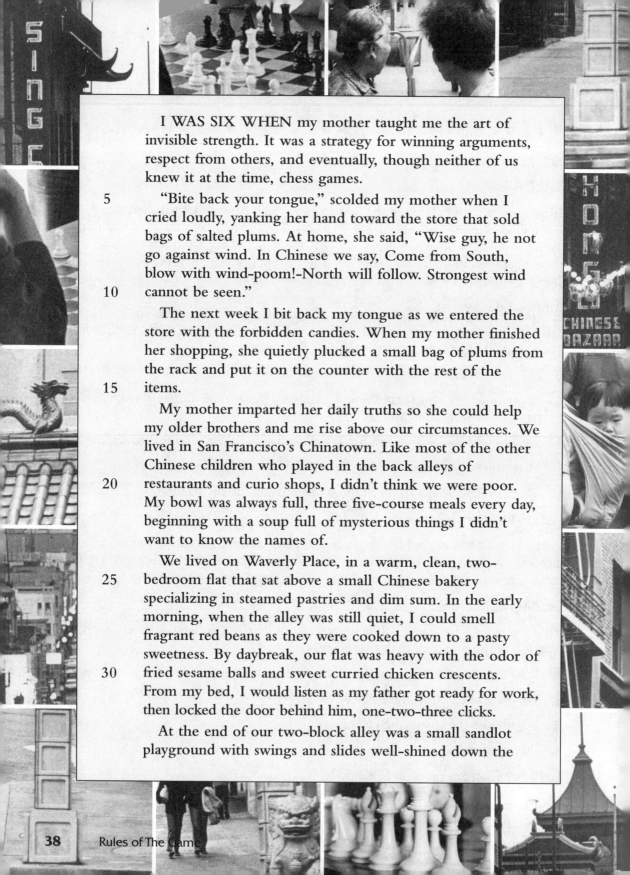

I WAS SIX WHEN my mother taught me the art of invisible strength. It was a strategy for winning arguments, respect from others, and eventually, though neither of us knew it at the time, chess games.

5   "Bite back your tongue," scolded my mother when I cried loudly, yanking her hand toward the store that sold bags of salted plums. At home, she said, "Wise guy, he not go against wind. In Chinese we say, Come from South, blow with wind-poom!-North will follow. Strongest wind
10   cannot be seen."

    The next week I bit back my tongue as we entered the store with the forbidden candies. When my mother finished her shopping, she quietly plucked a small bag of plums from the rack and put it on the counter with the rest of the
15   items.

    My mother imparted her daily truths so she could help my older brothers and me rise above our circumstances. We lived in San Francisco's Chinatown. Like most of the other Chinese children who played in the back alleys of
20   restaurants and curio shops, I didn't think we were poor. My bowl was always full, three five-course meals every day, beginning with a soup full of mysterious things I didn't want to know the names of.

    We lived on Waverly Place, in a warm, clean, two-
25   bedroom flat that sat above a small Chinese bakery specializing in steamed pastries and dim sum. In the early morning, when the alley was still quiet, I could smell fragrant red beans as they were cooked down to a pasty sweetness. By daybreak, our flat was heavy with the odor of
30   fried sesame balls and sweet curried chicken crescents. From my bed, I would listen as my father got ready for work, then locked the door behind him, one-two-three clicks.

    At the end of our two-block alley was a small sandlot playground with swings and slides well-shined down the

35　middle with use. The play area was bordered by wood-slat benches where old-country people sat cracking roasted watermelon seeds with their golden teeth and scattering the husks to an impatient gathering of gurgling pigeons. The best playground, however, was the dark alley itself. It was

40　crammed with daily mysteries and adventures. My brothers and I would peer into the medicinal herb shop, watching old Li dole out onto a stiff sheet of white paper the right amount of insect shells, saffron-colored seeds, and pungent leaves for his ailing customers. It was said that he once

45　cured a woman dying of an ancestral curse that had eluded the best of American doctors. Next to the pharmacy was a printer who specialized in gold-embossed wedding invitations and festive red banners.

　　Farther down the street was Ping Yuen Fish Market. The

50　front window displayed a tank crowded with doomed fish and turtles struggling to gain footing on the slimy green-tiled sides. A hand-written sign informed tourists, "Within this store, is all for food, not for pet." Inside, the butchers with their bloodstained white smocks deftly gutted the fish

55　while customers cried out their orders and shouted, "Give me your freshest," to which the butchers always protested, "All are freshest." On less crowded market days, we would inspect the crates of live frogs and crabs which we were warned not to poke, boxes of dried cuttlefish, and row

60　upon row of iced prawns, squid, and slippery fish. The sanddabs made me shiver each time; their eyes lay on one flattened side and reminded me of my mother's story of a careless girl who ran into a crowded street and was crushed by a cab. "Was smash flat," reported my mother.

65　　At the corner of the alley was Hong Sing's, a four-table cafe with a recessed stairwell in front that led to a door marked "Tradesmen." My brothers and I believed the bad people emerged from this door at night. Tourists never went

to Hong Sing's, since the menu was printed only in
Chinese. A Caucasian man with a big camera once posed
me and my playmates in front of the restaurant. He had us
move to the side of the picture window so the photo would
capture the roasted duck with its head dangling from a
juice-covered rope. After he took the picture, I told him he
should go into Hong Sing's and eat dinner. When he smiled
and asked me what they served, I shouted, "Guts and duck's
feet and octopus gizzards!" Then I ran off with my friends,
shrieking with laughter as we scampered across the alley
and hid in the entryway grotto of the China Gem Company,
my heart pounding with hope that he would chase us.

My mother named me after the street that we lived on:
Waverly Place Jong, my official name for important
American documents. But my family called me Meimei,
"Little Sister." I was the youngest, the only daughter. Each
morning before school, my mother would twist and yank
on my thick black hair until she had formed two tightly
wound pigtails. One day, as she struggled to weave a hard-
toothed comb through my disobedient hair, I had a sly
thought.

I asked her, "Ma, what is Chinese torture?" My mother
shook her head. A bobby pin was wedged between her lips.
She wetted her palm and smoothed the hair above my ear,
then pushed the pin in so that it nicked sharply against my
scalp.

"Who say this word?" she asked without a trace of
knowing how wicked I was being. I shrugged my shoulders
and said, "Some boy in my class said Chinese people do
Chinese torture."

"Chinese people do many things," she said simply.
"Chinese people do business, do medicine, do painting. Not
lazy like American people. We do torture. Best torture."

My older brother Vincent was the one who actually got

the chess set. We had gone to the annual Christmas party held at the First Chinese Baptist Church at the end of the alley. The missionary ladies had put together a Santa bag of gifts donated by members of another church. None of the gifts had names on them. There were separate sacks for boys and girls of different ages.

One of the Chinese parishioners had donned a Santa Claus costume and a stiff paper beard with cotton balls glued to it. I think the only children who thought he was the real thing were too young to know that Santa Claus was not Chinese. When my turn came up, the Santa man asked me how old I was. I thought it was a trick question; I was seven according to the American formula and eight by the Chinese calendar. I said I was born on March 17, 1951. That seemed to satisfy him. He then solemnly asked if I had been a very, very good girl this year and did I believe in Jesus Christ and obey my parents. I knew the only answer to that. I nodded back with equal solemnity.

Having watched the other children opening their gifts, I already knew that the big gifts were not necessarily the nicest ones. One girl my age got a large coloring book of biblical characters, while a less greedy girl who selected a smaller box received a glass vial of lavender toilet water. The sound of the box was also important. A ten-year-old boy had chosen a box that jangled when he shook it. It was a tin globe of the world with a slit for inserting money. He must have thought it was full of dimes and nickels, because when he saw that it had just ten pennies, his face fell with such undisguised disappointment that his mother slapped the side of his head and led him out of the church hall, apologizing to the crowd for her son who had such bad manners he couldn't appreciate such a fine gift.

As I peered into the sack, I quickly fingered the remaining presents, testing their weight, imagining what

they contained. I chose a heavy, compact one that was
wrapped in shiny silver foil and a red satin ribbon. It was a
twelve-pack of Life Savers and I spent the rest of the party
140 arranging and rearranging the candy tubes in the order of
my favorites. My brother Winston chose wisely as well. His
present turned out to be a box of intricate plastic parts; the
instructions on the box proclaimed that when they were
properly assembled he would have an authentic miniature
145 replica of a World War II submarine.

Vincent got the chess set, which would have been a very
decent present to get at a church Christmas party, except it
was obviously used and, as we discovered later, it was
missing a black pawn and a white knight. My mother
150 graciously thanked the unknown benefactor, saying, "Too
good. Cost too much." At which point, an old lady with
fine white, wispy hair nodded toward our family and said
with a whistling whisper, "Merry, merry Christmas."

When we got home, my mother told Vincent to throw
155 the chess set away. "She not want it. We not want it," she
said, tossing her head stiffly to the side with a tight, proud
smile. My brothers had deaf ears. They were already lining
up the chess pieces and reading from the dog-eared
instruction book.

160 I watched Vincent and Winston play during Christmas
week. The chessboard seemed to hold elaborate secrets
waiting to be untangled. The chessmen were more powerful
than Old Li's magic herbs that cured ancestral curses. And
my brothers wore such serious faces that I was sure
165 something was at stake that was greater than avoiding the
tradesmen's door to Hong Sing's.

"Let me! Let me!" I begged between games when one
brother or the other would sit back with a deep sigh of
relief and victory, the other annoyed, unable to let go of the
170 outcome. Vincent at first refused to let me play, but when I

offered my Life Savers as replacements for the buttons that filled in for the missing pieces, he relented. He chose the flavors: wild cherry for the black pawn and peppermint for the white knight. Winner could eat both.

175   As our mother sprinkled flour and rolled out small dough circles for the steamed dumplings that would be our dinner that night, Vincent explained the rules, pointing to each piece. "You have sixteen pieces and so do I. One king and queen, two bishops, two knights, two castles, and eight

180 pawns. The pawns can only move forward one step, except on the first move. Then they can move two. But they can only take men by moving crossways like this, except in the beginning, when you can move ahead and take another pawn."

185   "Why?" I asked as I moved my pawn. "Why can't they move more steps?"

    "Because they're pawns," he said.

    "But why do they go crossways to take other men? Why aren't there any women and children?"

190   "Why is the sky blue? Why must you always ask stupid questions?" asked Vincent. "This is a game. These are the rules. I didn't make them up. See. Here. In the book." He jabbed a page with a pawn in his hand. "Pawn. P-A-W-N. Pawn. Read it yourself."

195   My mother patted the flour off her hands. "Let me see book," she said quietly. She scanned the pages quickly, not reading the foreign English symbols, seeming to search deliberately for nothing in particular.

    "This American rules," she concluded at last. "Every time

200 people come out from foreign country, must know rules. You not know, judge say, Too bad, go back. They not telling you why so you can use their way go forward. They say, Don't know why, you find out yourself. But they

knowing all the time. Better you take it, find out why
205 yourself." She tossed her head back with a satisfied smile.

I found out about all the whys later. I read the rules and
looked up all the big words in a dictionary. I borrowed
books from the Chinatown library. I studied each chess
piece, trying to absorb the power each contained.

210 I learned about opening moves and why it's important to
control the center early on; the shortest distance between
two points is straight down the middle. I learned about the
middle game and why tactics between two adversaries are
like clashing ideas; the one who plays better has the clearest
215 plans for both attacking and getting out of traps. I learned
why it is essential in the endgame to have foresight, a
mathematical understanding of all possible moves, and
patience; all weaknesses and advantages become evident to
a strong adversary and are obscured to a tiring opponent. I
220 discovered that for the whole game one must gather
invisible strengths and see the endgame before the game
begins.

I also found out why I should never reveal "why" to
others. A little knowledge withheld is a great advantage one
225 should store for future use. That is the power of chess. It is
a game of secrets in which one must show and never tell.

I loved the secrets I found within the sixty-four black and
white squares. I carefully drew a handmade chessboard and
pinned it to the wall next to my bed, where at night I
230 would stare for hours at imaginary battles. Soon I no longer
lost any games or Life Savers, but I lost my adversaries.
Winston and Vincent decided they were more interested in
roaming the streets after school in their Hopalong Cassidy
cowboy hats.

235 On a cold spring afternoon, while walking home from
school, I detoured through the playground at the end of our
alley. I saw a group of old men, two seated across a folding

table playing a game of chess, others smoking pipes, eating peanuts, and watching. I ran home and grabbed Vincent's
240 chess set, which was bound in a cardboard box with rubber bands. I also carefully selected two prized rolls of Life Savers. I came back to the park and approached a man who was observing the game.

"Want to play?" I asked him. His face widened with
245 surprise and he grinned as he looked at the box under my arm.

"Little sister, been a long time since I play with dolls," he said, smiling benevolently. I quickly put the box down next to him on the bench and displayed my retort.

250 Lau Po, as he allowed me to call him, turned out to be a much better player than my brothers. I lost many games and many Life Savers. But over the weeks, with each diminishing roll of candies, I added new secrets. Lau Po gave me the names. The Double Attack from the East and
255 West Shores. Throwing Stones on the Drowning Man. The Sudden Meeting of the Clan. The Surprise from the Sleeping Guard. The Humble Servant Who Kills the King. Sand in the Eyes of Advancing Forces. A Double Killing Without Blood.

260 There were also the fine points of chess etiquette. Keep captured men in neat rows, as well-tended prisoners. Never announce "Check" with vanity, lest someone with an unseen sword slit your throat. Never hurl pieces into the sandbox after you have lost a game, because then you must
265 find them again, by yourself, after apologizing to all around you. By the end of the summer, Lau Po had taught me all he knew, and I had become a better chess player.

A small weekend crowd of Chinese people and tourists would gather as I played and defeated my opponents one by
270 one. My mother would join the crowds during these outdoor exhibition games. She sat proudly on the bench,

telling my admirers with proper Chinese humility, "Is luck."

A man who watched me play in the park suggested that my mother allow me to play in local chess tournaments. My mother smiled graciously, an answer that meant nothing. I desperately wanted to go, but I bit back my tongue. I knew she would not let me play among strangers. So as we walked home I said in a small voice that I didn't want to play in the local tournament. They would have American rules. If I lost, I would bring shame on my family.

"Is shame you fall down nobody push you," said my mother.

During my first tournament, my mother sat with me in the front row as I waited for my turn. I frequently bounced my legs to unstick them from the cold metal seat of the folding chair. When my name was called, I leapt up. My mother unwrapped something in her lap. It was her chang, a small tablet of red jade which held the sun's fire. "Is luck," she whispered, and tucked it into my dress pocket. I turned to my opponent, a fifteen-year-old boy from Oakland. He looked at me, wrinkling his nose.

As I began to play, the boy disappeared, the color ran out of the room, and I saw only my white pieces and his black ones waiting on the other side. A light wind began blowing past my ears. It whispered secrets only I could hear.

"Blow from the South," it murmured. "The wind leaves no trail." I saw a clear path, the traps to avoid. The crowd rustled. "Shhh! Shhh!" said the corners of the room. The wind blew stronger. "Throw sand from the East to distract him." The knight came forward ready for the sacrifice. The wind hissed, louder and louder. "Blow, blow, blow. He cannot see. He is blind now. Make him lean away from the wind so he is easier to knock down."

"Check," I said, as the wind roared with laughter. The wind died down to little puffs, my own breath.

My mother placed my first trophy next to a new plastic chess set that the neighborhood Tao society had given to me. As she wiped each piece with a soft cloth, she said, "Next time win more, lose less."

310   "Ma, it's not how many pieces you lose," I said. "Sometimes you need to lose pieces to get ahead."

"Better to lose less, see if you really need."

At the next tournament, I won again, but it was my mother who wore the triumphant grin.

315   "Lost eight piece this time. Last time was eleven. What I tell you? Better off lose less!" I was annoyed, but I couldn't say anything.

I attended more tournaments, each one farther away from home. I won all games, in all divisions. The Chinese bakery

320   downstairs from our flat displayed my growing collection of trophies in its window, amidst the dust-covered cakes that were never picked up. The day after I won an important regional tournament, the window encased a fresh sheet cake with whipped-cream frosting and red script saying

325   "Congratulations, Waverly Jong, Chinatown Chess Champion." Soon after that, a flower shop, headstone engraver, and funeral parlor offered to sponsor me in national tournaments. That's when my mother decided I no longer had to do the dishes. Winston and Vincent had to

330   do my chores.

"Why does she get to play and we do all the work," complained Vincent.

"Is new American rules," said my mother. "Meimei play, squeeze all her brains out for win chess. You play, worth

335   squeeze towel."

By my ninth birthday, I was a national chess champion. I was still some 429 points away from grand-master status, but I was touted as the Great American Hope, a child

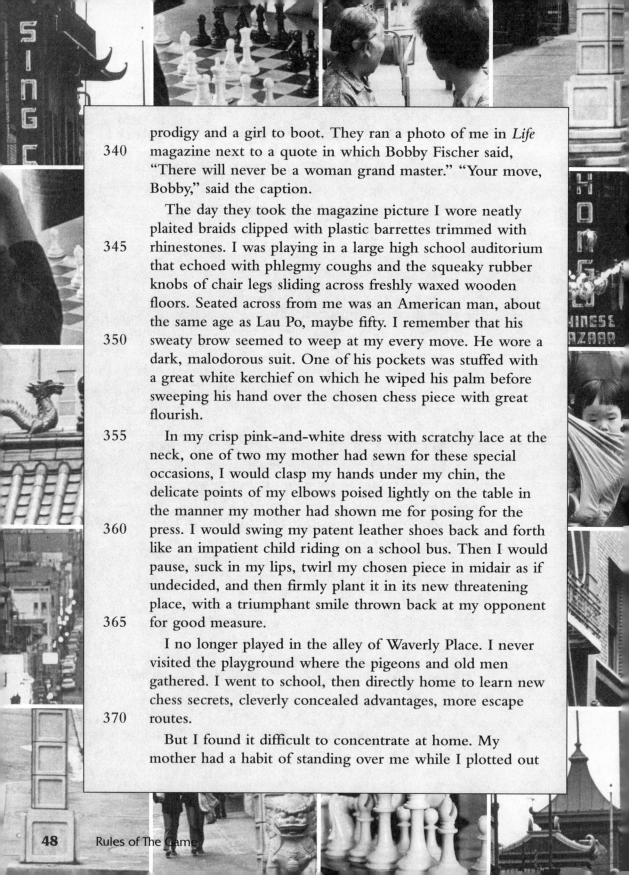

prodigy and a girl to boot. They ran a photo of me in *Life*
340 magazine next to a quote in which Bobby Fischer said,
"There will never be a woman grand master." "Your move,
Bobby," said the caption.

The day they took the magazine picture I wore neatly
plaited braids clipped with plastic barrettes trimmed with
345 rhinestones. I was playing in a large high school auditorium
that echoed with phlegmy coughs and the squeaky rubber
knobs of chair legs sliding across freshly waxed wooden
floors. Seated across from me was an American man, about
the same age as Lau Po, maybe fifty. I remember that his
350 sweaty brow seemed to weep at my every move. He wore a
dark, malodorous suit. One of his pockets was stuffed with
a great white kerchief on which he wiped his palm before
sweeping his hand over the chosen chess piece with great
flourish.

355 In my crisp pink-and-white dress with scratchy lace at the
neck, one of two my mother had sewn for these special
occasions, I would clasp my hands under my chin, the
delicate points of my elbows poised lightly on the table in
the manner my mother had shown me for posing for the
360 press. I would swing my patent leather shoes back and forth
like an impatient child riding on a school bus. Then I would
pause, suck in my lips, twirl my chosen piece in midair as if
undecided, and then firmly plant it in its new threatening
place, with a triumphant smile thrown back at my opponent
365 for good measure.

I no longer played in the alley of Waverly Place. I never
visited the playground where the pigeons and old men
gathered. I went to school, then directly home to learn new
chess secrets, cleverly concealed advantages, more escape
370 routes.

But I found it difficult to concentrate at home. My
mother had a habit of standing over me while I plotted out

my games. I think she thought of herself as my protective ally. Her lips would be sealed tight, and after each move I
375 made, a soft "Hmmmmph" would escape from her nose.

"Ma, I can't practice when you stand there like that," I said one day. She retreated to the kitchen and made loud noises with the pots and pans. When the crashing stopped, I could see out of the corner of my eye that she was
380 standing in the doorway. "Hmmmph!" Only this one came out of her tight throat.

My parents made many concessions to allow me to practice. One time I complained that the bedroom I shared was so noisy that I couldn't think. Thereafter, my brothers
385 slept in a bed in the living room facing the street. I said I couldn't finish my rice; my head didn't work right when my stomach was too full. I left the table with half-finished bowls and nobody complained. But there was one duty I couldn't avoid. I had to accompany my mother on Saturday
390 market days when I had no tournament to play. My mother would proudly walk with me, visiting many shops, buying very little. "This my daughter Wave-ly Jong," she said to whoever looked her way.

One day after we left a shop I said under my breath, "I
395 wish you wouldn't do that, telling everybody I'm your daughter." My mother stopped walking. Crowds of people with heavy bags pushed past us on the sidewalk, bumping into first one shoulder, then another.

"Aiii-ya. So shame be with mother?" She grasped my
400 hand even tighter as she glared at me.

I looked down. "It's not that, it's just so obvious. It's just so embarrassing."

"Embarrass you be my daughter?" Her voice was cracking with anger.
405 "That's not what I meant. That's not what I said."

"What you say?"

I knew it was a mistake to say anything more, but I heard my voice speaking, "Why do you have to use me to show off? If you want to show off, then why don't you learn to play chess?"

My mother's eyes turned into dangerous black slits. She had no words for me, just sharp silence.

I felt the wind rushing around my hot ears. I jerked my hand out of my mother's tight grasp and spun around, knocking into an old woman. Her bag of groceries spilled to the ground.

"Aii-ya! Stupid girl!" my mother and the woman cried. Oranges and tin cans careened down the sidewalk. As my mother stooped to help the old woman pick up the escaping food, I took off.

I raced down the street, dashing between people, not looking back as my mother screamed shrilly, "Meimei! Meimei!" I fled down an alley, past dark, curtained shops and merchants washing the grime off their windows. I sped into the sunlight, into a large street crowded with tourists examining trinkets and souvenirs. I ducked into another dark alley, down another street, up another alley. I ran until it hurt and I realized I had nowhere to go, that I was not running from anything. The alleys contained no escape routes.

My breath came out like angry smoke. It was cold. I sat down on an upturned plastic pail next to a stack of empty boxes, cupping my chin with my hands, thinking hard. I imagined my mother, first walking briskly down one street or another looking for me, then giving up and returning home to await my arrival. After two hours, I stood up on creaking legs and slowly walked home.

The alley was quiet and I could see the yellow lights shining from our flat like two tiger's eyes in the night. I climbed the sixteen steps to the door, advancing quietly up

440 each so as not to make any warning sounds. I turned the knob; the door was locked. I heard a chair moving, quick steps, the locks turning–click! click! click!–and then the door opened.

"About time you got home," said Vincent. "Boy, are you
445 in trouble."

He slid back to the dinner table. On a platter were the remains of a large fish, its fleshy head still connected to bones swimming upstream in vain escape. Standing there waiting for my punishment, I heard my mother speak in a
450 dry voice.

"We not concerning this girl. This girl not have concerning for us."

Nobody looked at me. Bone chopsticks clinked against the inside of bowls being emptied into hungry mouths.

455 I walked into my room, closed the door, and lay down on my bed. The room was dark, the ceiling filled with shadows from the dinnertime lights of neighboring flats.

In my head, I saw a chessboard with sixty-four black and white squares. Opposite me was my opponent, two angry
460 black slits. She wore a triumphant smile. "Strongest wind cannot be seen," she said.

Her black men advanced across the plane, slowly marching to each successive level as a single unit. My white pieces screamed as they scurried and fell off the board one by one.
465 As her men drew closer to my edge, I felt myself growing light. I rose up into the air and flew out the window. Higher and higher, above the alley, over the tops of tiled roofs, where I was gathered up by the wind and pushed up toward the night sky until everything below me disappeared and I
470 was alone.

I closed my eyes and pondered my next move.

Rules of the Game

Glossary

to yank	to pull sharply
to impart	to give
fragrant	good-smelling
to scatter	to spread
a husk	the hard covering of a seed
to gurgle	to make a soft sound deep in the throat
crammed with	filled with
to peer	to look with difficulty
to dole out	to measure out
pungent	strong smelling
ancestral curse	a call from ancient times for evil to come upon a family
deftly	skillfully
to gut	to take out the insides of something (like a fish)
to shriek	to scream
to scamper	to run very quickly and lightly as a child
sly	secretive, cunning,
bobby pin	a thin pin to hold the hair back
solemn	serious
greedy	showing too much desire (as for food or money)
Life Savers	small round candies of different colors and flavors
benefactor	someone who gives help (money) to others
dog-eared	describing the corners of book pages which have been turned down
elaborate	complicated

the outcome	the result
adversary	enemy, opponent
to clash	to conflict, to disagree strongly
to obscure	to hide
benevolent	kind
retort	quick answer
etiquette	manners, proper style
vanity	pride
humility	not proud
triumphant	rejoicing at success
annoyed	bothered, or a little angry
chores	daily household tasks
a child prodigy	a child with wonderful abilities beyond his or her age
malodorous	bad smelling
ally	a person who cooperates with someone in a project (as in war)
concession	some special thing which someone allows
slit	tiny opening
to careen	to move quickly over to one side
to scurry	to run very quickly, like a mouse

Comprehension Check

Complete the following sentences in your own words.

1. We know the Jong family was not rich because _____.

2. Vincent got a chess set at _____.

3. Waverly's brothers stop playing chess with her because _____.

4. Waverly learns chess techniques from _____.

5. Mrs. Jong _____ understand(s) how to play chess.

6. This story covers about _____ years.

7. It was difficult for Waverly to concentrate at home because _____.

8. Waverly finds the Saturday walk through the market with her mother very _____

   _____.

9. Mrs. Jong punishes Waverly's outburst at the market by _____.

10. At the end of the story, Waverly lies in bed and imagines that she is _____

    _____.

Comprehension Check: Plot Summary

The teacher will divide you into three groups. Each group should appoint a group secretary. Write a group summary of the story, with a maximum number of 70 words. Then pass on your group summary to another group, who will rewrite it to half its length (35 words). This reduced summary is passed again to the third group who reduces its length to about 15 to 20 words. Each group should read their final version out loud.

Word Study: Synonyms

Match the following words with the appropriate synonyms from the story.

1.	(page 38, paragraph 2)	pulling	_____
2.	(page 39, paragraph 2)	full of	_____
3.	(40, 1)	screaming	_____
4.	(42, 1)	copy (noun)	_____
5.	(42, last)	asked	_____
6.	(44, 3)	enemy	_____
7.	(45, 3)	kindly	_____
8.	(47, 4)	proud	_____
9.	(48, 3)	hold	_____
10.	(49, 3)	privileges	_____
11.	(49, 5)	held	_____
12.	(51, last)	thought about	_____

Most of these synonyms have a slightly different nuance. Use a dictionary to find the shared meanings and the different nuances.

Interpretation

1. In the first three pages, Tan sets up a rich atmosphere of the Jong family home. What phrases or adjectives help to create the tone? How would you describe this tone?

2. We see Waverly from ages 6 to 9. List three important events or time periods that mark her ability to "bite back her tongue" as she grows up.

3. Although Waverly says, "I no longer played in the alley," in the end she runs away to the alley. a. Find references to the alley. Why is it important to Waverly? What was your favorite place as a child and why?

   b. Waverly studies chess strategies to learn "more escape routes" (p. 48). However, when she runs away to the alley, she discovers the "alley contained no escape routes" (p. 50). Why does Tan compare chess and the alley this way?

4. How is the quarrel between Mrs. Jong and Waverly like a chess game? Find three words that are also used in the game of chess (p. 50–51) . What is Mrs. Jong's surprise "strategy" when Waverly returns home?

5. The story was originally called "Endgame." Why? Which title do you prefer?

Evaluation: Discussion or Response Journal

1. What "rules of the game" does Waverly discover? Do you think these are universal rules, strong in every culture? In your culture?

2. Whom do you admire most, Mrs. Jong or Waverly? Why?

3. What will be Waverly's "next move"?

4. Re-read the first paragraph. Do you agree with what Mrs. Jong tries to teach her daughter?

A Moving Day

by Susan Nunes

"How do we choose among what we experience, what we are taught, what we run into by chance, or what is forced upon us?"

Background:

This nostalgic story moves between time frames until the reader finally builds up an understanding of the main character, the mother's, past life. The mother's experience and character is starkly and finely drawn by the end of the story. Nunes eloquently expresses the inevitability of old age, the crumbling of the past, and the power of the present.

Warm-up Discussion/Response Journal:

- What do you think of when you hear the title "A Moving Day"? What emotions does the title bring?

- Does your family have any heirlooms? Do you wish to have them someday? Why or why not?

- Do you think it is important to pass on traditions from generation to generation? Why or why not?

- Is your culture a very "traditional" one? Give examples of how it keeps traditions, yet takes on new ones.

Guiding Questions:

Read the story once quickly. It is not necessary that you understand every word. Just concentrate on getting the main ideas.

1. **Who** are the main characters? What do you know about them?

2. **Where** does the story take place?

3. **When** does the story take place?

4. **What** happens?

5. **What changes** occur in the story?

ACROSS THE STREET, the bulldozer roars to life. Distracted, my mother looks up from the pile of embroidered linen that she has been sorting. She is seventy, tiny and fragile, the flesh burned off her shrinking frame.

5 Her hair is gray now—she had never dyed it—and she wears it cut close to her head with the nape shaved. Her natural hairline would have been better suited to the kimono worn by women of her mother's generation. She still has a beautiful neck. In recent years she has taken a liking to

10 jeans, cotton smocks, baggy sweaters, and running shoes. When I was a child she wouldn't have been caught dead without her nylons.

Her hands, now large-jointed with arthritis, return to the pile of linen. Her movements always had a no-nonsense

15 quality and ever since I was a child, I have been wary of her energy because it was so often driven by suppressed anger. Now she is making two stacks, the larger one for us, the smaller for her to keep. There is a finality in the way she places things in the larger pile, as if to say that's *it*. For

20 her, it's all over, all over but this last accounting. She does not look forward to what is coming. Strangers. Schedules. The regulated activities of those considered too old to regulate themselves. But at least, at the *very* least, she'll not be a burden. She sorts through the possessions of a

25 lifetime, she and her three daughters. It's time she passed most of this on. Dreams are lumber. She can't *wait* to be rid of them.

My two sisters and I present a contrast. There is nothing purposeful or systematic about the way we move. In fact,

30 we don't know where we're going. We know there is a message in all this activity, but we don't know what it is. Still, we search for it in the odd carton, between layers of

tissue paper and silk. We open drawers, peer into the
recesses of cupboards, rummage through the depths of
35   closets. What a lot of stuff! We lift, untuck, unwrap, and
set aside. The message is there, we know. But what is it?
Perhaps if we knew, then we wouldn't have to puzzle out
our mother's righteous determination to shed the past.

There is a photograph of my mother taken on the porch
40   of my grandparents' house when she was in her twenties.
She is wearing a floral print dress with a square, lace-edged
collar and a graceful skirt that shows off her slim body.
Her shoulder-length hair has been permed. It is dark and
thick and worn parted on the side to fall over her right
45   cheek. She is very fair; "one pound powder," her friends
called her. She is smiling almost reluctantly, as if she meant
to appear serious but the photographer has said something
amusing. One arm rests lightly on the railing, the other,
which is at her side, holds a handkerchief. They were her
50   special pleasures, handkerchiefs of hand-embroidered linen
as fine as rice paper. Most were gifts (she used to say that
when she was a girl, people gave one another little things–a
handkerchief, a pincushion, pencils, hair ribbons), and she
washed and starched them by hand, ironed them, taking
55   care with the rolled hems, and stored them in a silk bag
from Japan.

There is something expectant in her stance, as if she
were waiting for something to happen. She says, your
father took this photograph in 1940, before we were
60   married. She lowers her voice confidentially and adds, now
he cannot remember taking it. My father sits on the
balcony, an open book on his lap, peacefully smoking his
pipe. The bulldozer tears into the foundations of the
Kitamura house.

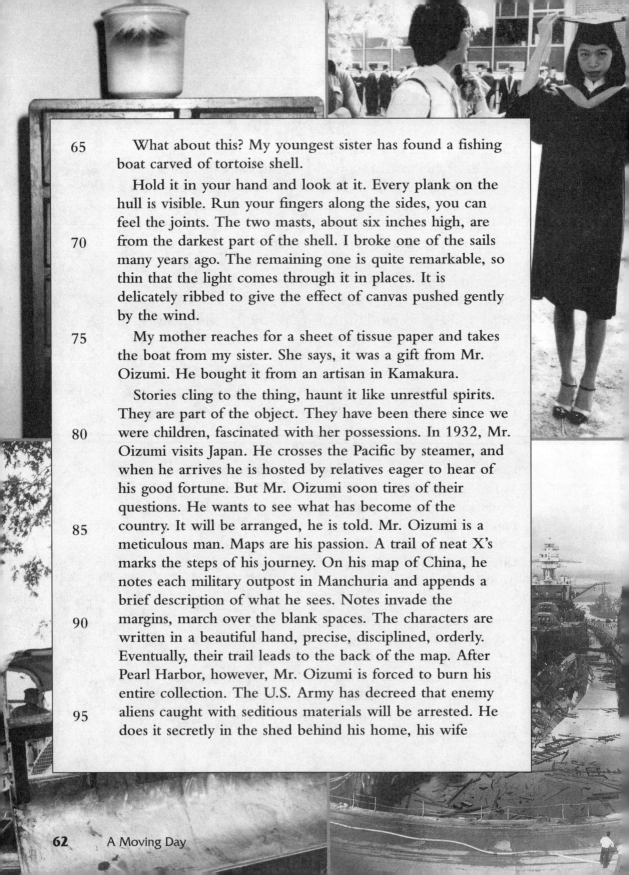

65   What about this? My youngest sister has found a fishing boat carved of tortoise shell.

Hold it in your hand and look at it. Every plank on the hull is visible. Run your fingers along the sides, you can feel the joints. The two masts, about six inches high, are

70   from the darkest part of the shell. I broke one of the sails many years ago. The remaining one is quite remarkable, so thin that the light comes through it in places. It is delicately ribbed to give the effect of canvas pushed gently by the wind.

75   My mother reaches for a sheet of tissue paper and takes the boat from my sister. She says, it was a gift from Mr. Oizumi. He bought it from an artisan in Kamakura.

Stories cling to the thing, haunt it like unrestful spirits. They are part of the object. They have been there since we

80   were children, fascinated with her possessions. In 1932, Mr. Oizumi visits Japan. He crosses the Pacific by steamer, and when he arrives he is hosted by relatives eager to hear of his good fortune. But Mr. Oizumi soon tires of their questions. He wants to see what has become of the

85   country. It will be arranged, he is told. Mr. Oizumi is a meticulous man. Maps are his passion. A trail of neat X's marks the steps of his journey. On his map of China, he notes each military outpost in Manchuria and appends a brief description of what he sees. Notes invade the

90   margins, march over the blank spaces. The characters are written in a beautiful hand, precise, disciplined, orderly. Eventually, their trail leads to the back of the map. After Pearl Harbor, however, Mr. Oizumi is forced to burn his entire collection. The U.S. Army has decreed that enemy

95   aliens caught with seditious materials will be arrested. He does it secretly in the shed behind his home, his wife

standing guard. They scatter the ashes in the garden among the pumpkin vines.

My grandfather's library does not escape the flames either.
100 After the army requisitions the Japanese school for wartime headquarters, they give my mother's parents twenty-four hours to vacate the premises, including the boarding house where they lived with about twenty students from the plantation camps outside Hilo. There is no time to save the
105 books. Her father decides to nail wooden planks over the shelves that line the classrooms. After the army moves in, they rip open the planks, confiscate the books, and store them in the basement of the post office. Later, the authorities burn everything. Histories, children's stories,
110 primers, biographies, language texts, everything, even a set of Encyclopaedia Brittanica. My grandfather is shipped to Oahu and imprisoned on Sand Island. A few months later, he is released after three prominent Caucasians vouch for his character. It is a humiliation he doesn't speak of, ever.

115 All of this was part of the boat. After I broke the sail, she gathered the pieces and said, I'm not sure we can fix this. It was not a toy. Why can't you leave my things alone?

For years the broken boat sat on our bookshelf, a reminder of the brutality of the next generation.

120 Now she wants to give everything away. We have to beg her to keep things. Dishes from Japan, lacquerware, photographs, embroidery, letters. She says, I have no room. You take them, here, *take* them. Take them or I'll get rid of them.

125 They're piled around her, they fill storage chests, they fall out of open drawers and cupboards. She only wants to keep a few things—her books, some photographs, three carved wooden figures from Korea that belonged to her father, a

few of her mother's dishes, perhaps one futon.

130 My sister holds a porcelain teapot by its bamboo handle. Four white cranes edged in black and gold fly around it. She asks, Mama, can't you hang on to this? If you keep it, I can borrow it later.

My mother shakes her head. She is adamant. And what
135 would I do with it? I don't want any of this. Really.

My sister turns to me. She sighs. The situation is hopeless. You take it, she says. It'll only get broken at my place. The kids.

It had begun slowly, this shedding of the past, a plate
140 here, a dish there, a handkerchief, a doily, a teacup, a few photographs, one of my grandfather's block prints. Nothing big. But then the odd gesture became a pattern; it got so we never left the house empty-handed. At first we were amused. After all, when we were children she had to fend
145 us off her things. Threaten. We were always *at* them. She had made each one so ripe with memories that we found them impossible to resist. We snuck them outside, showed them to our friends, told and retold the stories. They bear the scars of all this handling, even her most personal
150 possessions. A chip here, a crack there. Casualties. Like the music box her brother brought home from Italy after the war. It played a Brahms lullaby. First we broke the spring, then we lost the winding key, and for years it sat mutely on her dresser.

She would say again and again, it's impossible to keep
155 anything nice with you children. And we'd retreat, wounded, for a while. The problem with children is they can wipe out your history. It's a miracle that anything survives this onslaught.

There's a photograph of my mother standing on the pier
160 in Honolulu in 1932, the year she left Hawaii to attend the

University of California. She's loaded to the ears with leis. She's wearing a fedora pulled smartly to the side. She's not smiling. Of my mother's two years there, my grandmother recalled that she received good grades and never wore a

165   kimono again. My second cousin, with whom my mother stayed when she first arrived, said she was surprisingly sophisticated—she liked hats. My mother said that she was homesick. Her favorite class was biology and she entertained ambitions of becoming a scientist. Her father, however,

170   wanted her to become a teacher, and his wishes prevailed, even though he would not have forced them upon her. She was a dutiful daughter.

    During her second year, she lived near campus with a mathematics professor and his wife. In exchange for room

175   and board she cleaned house, ironed, and helped prepare meals. One of the things that survives from this period is a black composition book entitled *Recipes of California*. As a child, I read it like a book of mysteries for clues to a life which seemed both alien and familiar. Some entries she had

180   copied by hand; others she cut out of magazines and pasted on the page, sometimes with a picture or drawing. The margins contained her cryptic comments: "Saturday bridge club," "From Mary G. Do not give away," underlined, "chopped suet by hand, wretched task, bed at 2 A.M.,

185   exhausted." I remember looking up "artichoke" in the dictionary and asking Mr. Okinaga, the vegetable vendor, if he had any edible thistles. I never ate one until I was sixteen.

    That book holds part of the answer to why our family

190   rituals didn't fit the recognized norm of either our relatives or the larger community in which we grew up. At home, we ate in fear of the glass of spilled milk, the stray elbow on the table, the boarding house reach. At my grandparents',

we slurped our *chasuke*. We wore tailored dresses, white
cotton pinafores, and Buster Brown shoes with white socks;
however, what we longed for were the lacy, ornate dresses
in the National Dollar Store that the Puerto Rican girls
wore to church on Sunday. For six years, I marched to
Japanese language school after my regular classes; however,
we only spoke English at home. We talked too loudly and
all at once, which mortified my mother, but she was always
complaining about Japanese indirectness. I know that she
smarted under a system in which the older son is the center
of the familial universe, but at thirteen I had a fit of jealous
rage over her fawning attention to our only male cousin.

My sister has found a photograph of my mother, a round-
faced and serious twelve or thirteen, dressed in a kimono
and seated, on her knees, on the *tatami* floor. She is playing
the *koto*. According to my mother, girls were expected to
learn this difficult stringed instrument because it was
thought to teach discipline. Of course, everything Japanese
was a lesson in discipline–flower arranging, calligraphy, judo,
brush painting, embroidery, everything. One summer my
sister and I had to take *ikebana*, the art of flower
arrangement, at Grandfather's school. The course was taught
by Mrs. Oshima, a diminutive, soft-spoken, terrifying
woman, and my supplies were provided by my grandmother,
whose tastes ran to the oversized. I remember little of that
class and its principles. What I remember most clearly is
having to walk home carrying, in a delicate balancing act,
one of our creations, which, more often than not, towered
above our heads.

How do we choose among what we experience, what we
are taught, what we run into by chance, or what is forced
upon us? What is the principle of selection? My sisters and I
are not bound by any of our mother's obligations, nor do we
follow the rituals that seemed so important. My sister once

asked, do you realize that when she's gone that's *it*? She was talking about how to make sushi, but it was a profound question nonetheless.

230

I remember, after we moved to Honolulu and my mother stopped teaching and began working long hours in administration, she was less vigilant about the many little things that once consumed her attention. While we didn't exactly slide into savagery, we economized in more ways than one. She would often say, there's simply no time anymore to do things right.

235

I didn't understand then why she looked so sad when she said it, but somehow I knew the comment applied to us. It would be terrible if centuries of culture are lost simply because there is not time.

240

Still, I don't understand why we carry out this fruitless search. Whatever it is we are looking for, we're not going to find it. My sister tries to lift a box filled with record albums, old seventy-eights, gives up, and sets it down again. My mothers says, there are people who collect these things. Imagine.

245

Right, just imagine.

I think about my mother bathing me and singing, "The snow is snowing, the wind is blowing, but I will weather the storm." And I think of her story of the village boy carried by the Tengu on a fantastic flight over the cities of Japan, but who returns to a disbelieving and resistant family. So much for questions which have no answers, why we look among objects for meanings which have somehow escaped us in the growing up and growing old.

250

255

However, my mother is a determined woman. She will take nothing with her if she can help it. It is all ours. And on the balcony my father knocks the ashes of his pipe into a porcelain ashtray, and the bulldozer is finally silent.

260

A Moving Day

Glossary

distracted	to have one's attention caught or broken
fragile	small, weak, easy to break
to shrink	to get smaller
arthritis	a condition causing pain and stiffness in the joints, often in the hands
wary	careful, afraid
suppressed	hidden, kept from being seen
lumber	1) (noun) wood cut into long flat pieces; 2) (verb) to move in a heavy way
righteous	making a show of doing what is right
reluctantly	unwilling, not wanting to do something
confidential	to be kept secret
to cling	to hold tightly
to append	to add
seditious	going against the government's authority
to requisition	to officially make use of property or materials
to confiscate	to officially take away
to vouch for	to support, to guarantee the truth of something
humiliation	shame
brutality	violence, cruelty
adamant	quite sure, unyielding
to shed	to remove, layer by layer
to sneak	to go or take secretly
mutely	silently
onslaught	an attack
lei	a garland of flowers worn around the neck, well-known in Hawaii
fedora	a type of hat

"the boarding house reach" (idiom)	to stretch rudely across the table to take some food
to slurp	to drink (or eat something like soup) noisily
to mortify	to embarass, to shame
to smart under	to suffer
tatami floor	Japanese floor made of rice straw
diminutive	small
sushi	Japanese food, pieces of raw fish put on or rolled in small squares of rice
vigilant	watching carefully
fruitless	useless

Comprehension Check

This poetic story may be confusing after only one reading because it does not follow a logical time order. There are many "flashbacks," when the narrator goes back into time, but sometimes the verb tense does not change from the present to the past tense. It is as if we are following the mind of the narrator as she skips from one thought in the present to another thought in the past. The following exercise should help you to organize the events of the story in chronological order. The events are not in the correct time order. Number them from earliest (1) to most recent (11). The first and last ones are done for you.

___ Grandpa is imprisoned on Sand Island for a few months.

_1_ Mother leaves Hawaii to attend the University of California (1932).

___ Mother begins to give away her prized possessions.

___ Mother and Father and their daughters move from Hilo to Honolulu.

___ Mother and Father get married.

___ Grandpa's library is burned by American military.

___ Mother stops teaching.

___ Grandma and Grandpa vacate the Japanese school they ran near Hilo, Hawaii.

_11_ Mother and Father prepare to move into an old age home (around 1985-1990).

___ Mother begins wearing only Western clothes.

___ Japanese bomb Pearl Harbor.

Comprehension Check: Plot Summary

Using the eleven sentences above, write a summary of the events of Mother's life. You should connect the sentences with transitions like "then," "although," "however," "finally," etc., and you should add some phrases of your own to make the summary smooth and meaningful.

The first sentence is done for you:

> The story of Mother's life, as told in this short story, *A Moving Day*, begins when Mother leaves Hawaii in 1932 to attend the University of California. It is during her university years that...

Vocabulary: Word Forms

Change the word form as necessary to complete the sentence correctly. After you have completed the sentences, check back with the text to see if your answers are correct.

1. distract   _____, the mother looked up from her housework.
   (page 60)

2. purpose   There is nothing _____ about the way the three sisters
   (page 60)   move.

3. delicate   It is _____ ribbed to give the effect of canvas pushed by the
   (page 62)   wind.

4. brutal   For years the broken boat sat on the bookshelf, a reminder of the
   (page 63)   _____ of the next generation.

5. stand   There's a photo of my mother _____ on the pier in Honolulu.
   (page 64)

6. complain   She _____ always _____ about Japanese indirectness.
   (page 66)

7. walk   What I remember is having _____ home carrying one of our
   (page 66)   creations.

Interpretation

1. What is the significance of the title? Who is moving? Where? Check your dictionary for other possible meanings of the word "moving."

2. The new generation, children, are described as violently destroying the past. Find three sentences in the story that demonstrate this. Do you think this is a fair and realistic description?

3. Mother seems to treasure the past and want to remain "Japanese," yet also desires to become Westernized. Find two examples of these conflicting desires.

4. Does the narrator share the same conflicts as her mother?

5. "Ever since I was a child, I have been wary of her energy because it was so often driven by suppressed anger." (p.60). What may be the source of Mother's anger?

6. "I think of her story of the village boy carried by the Tengu," This refers to an old Japanese folk tale about Tengu, a goblin with a huge nose. He used an enormous leaf in order to fly, and sometimes kidnapped children, taking them on a flight around Japan. When the children returned to their families, they were generally not believed; however, sometimes the children acquired special skills (like being able to communicate with animals) on their trip. Why might this be a favorite story of Mother's?

7. Explain the symbolism of the last line: "And on the balcony my father knocks the ashes of his pipe into a porcelain ashtray and the bulldozer is finally silent."

8. "Still I don't understand why we carry out this fruitless search." (p.67). What are they looking for, and why is it a fruitless search?

Evaluation: Discussion or Response Journal

1. Is this a sad or happy story?

2. What are the conflicts of this story? Are they inevitable?

3. How would you describe Mother?

4. What is your attitude toward Mother? Admiring? Critical? Puzzled?

Sadie and Maud

by Gwendolyn Brooks

"Maud went to college. Sadie stayed at home."

PRE-READING

The first two lines of this poem are:

Maud went to college.

Sadie stayed at home.

With your partner, imagine the character and the future lives of these two sisters, Maud and Sadie.

Discuss the value of college and university education in your culture and in your own family. Is going to college always a good idea? Will you go to college? Why or why not? If you are in college now, why?

Listen as your teacher reads aloud the first four stanzas.

- What kind of person is Sadie?

- What kind of people are Maud, Ma, and Papa?

- What kind of people are Sadie's children?

- What do you think happens to Maud?

Now listen to the final stanza about Maud. Are you surprised?

Sadie and Maud

1   Maud went to college.
     Sadie stayed at home.
     Sadie scraped life
     With a fine-tooth comb.

2   She didn't leave a tangle in.
     Her comb found every strand.
     Sadie was one of the livingest chits
     In all the land.

3   Sadie bore two babies
     Under her maiden name.
     Maud and Ma and Papa
     Nearly died of shame.

4   When Sadie said her last so-long
     Her girls struck out from home.
     (Sadie had left as heritage
     Her fine-tooth comb.)

5   Maud, who went to college,
     Is a thin brown mouse.
     She is living all alone
     In this old house.

Gwendolyn Brooks

Glossary

to scrape	to rub a surface with great pressure, in order to smooth, remove, or injure the surface
a fine-tooth comb	a plastic instrument with closely spaced teeth used to smooth the hair
a tangle	a confused mess; in this case, a knot in hair
a chit	a bold, lively girl
to bear (past tense, bore)	to give birth (have a baby)
maiden name	unmarried name
so-long (informal)	good-bye
to strike out from (idiom)	to leave in order to begin a difficult journey

POETIC FEATURES

a. Coinage

When a writer "coins" a word or phrase, she or he invents it. That is, the writer makes up a word, often modifying a known word to suit her or his purpose. Find an example of coinage in stanza 2 of this poem. Define the new word.

b. Figurative Language: Metaphors

A metaphor is a comparison of two things without using the word "like" or "as." For example: Your fingers are sausages.

Examine the following metaphors. What two things are being compared, and why?

1. Maud is a thin brown mouse.

2. Sadie scraped life with a fine-tooth comb. She didn't leave a tangle in. Her comb found every strand.

THEME

What is Sadie's philosophy of life? Maud's? Sadie's children's? Which philosophy do you think the poet is most sympathetic with? How do you know this? Which philosophy are you most sympathetic with?

CHORAL READING

In groups of three or four, prepare a "choral reading" of the poem. The choral reading is a dramatic reading, and the purpose is for your group to read the poem in such a way that its tone and meaning are clear to the audience.

When you read it as a group, you may have everyone read all of the lines together, or give certain people certain parts. Vary the volume, speed, and emphasis. When you are ready, perform it for the class.

CLASS WRITING ACTIVITY

Half the class is Maud; the other half, one of Sadie's daughters. Sadie has died, and the daughters have already left home.

Maud: In small groups, compose a letter of advice to Sadie's daughters (your nieces). When you have finished, exchange with a group that is taking the identity of the daughters.

Sadie's daughters: In small groups, compose a letter of advice to your Aunt Maud. When you have finished, exchange with a group that is taking the identity of Maud.

Leg. Reunion
Sadie + Maud

UNIT 2 PROJECTS:

I. Just A Minute: (10 to 15 minute review of character)

In this activity, try to speak for 15 seconds on a given topic - in this case, a character, without hesitation or repetition.

Roger or Mrs. Jones (*Thank You, M'am*)

Frank (*Leg*)

Charlie or Charlie's father (*Reunion*)

Mrs. Jong or Waverly (*Rules of the Game*)

Mother or Daughter/Narrator (*A Moving Day*)

Sadie or Maud ("Sadie and Maud")

Warm-up: Each group (three to five students) has a bag with character's names written on slips of paper. As each member pulls a slip, he or she must talk about the character for 15 seconds, at which point the teacher calls time, and the next person draws a new character's name. Help your group members as needed.

Relay: Each group is a team. When the teacher pulls a slip and says a character's name, one student from each team talks about the character for 15 seconds, at which point the teacher calls time, and the next person in that team takes over talking about the same character. The team which completes one full minute gets 4 points. If one member stops before 15 seconds, then the team must sit down.

II. Oral Character Analysis: Small Group Presentation

This is a "semi-formal" speaking assignment. You will choose one character from the stories in Units One or Two and speak for about 5 to 8 minutes about his or her character. You will give your presentation to a group of 3 students. After you finish speaking, you will lead a five-minute discussion about the character you chose, with prepared questions.

Remember that characters are developed by the author's description, character's action and speech, and other's reaction to the character. You need to present two or three characteristics and give specific examples from the story that show these characteristics.

This is called "semi-formal" because you will be speaking only to a few people, and it will involve discussion as well as your speech. You must be very organized, however, by making "presentation cards" which outline the introduction, body, and conclusion of your talk. You will also need to outline questions for the five minute discussion. You must speak, *not* read from the notes on your cards.

1. ORGANIZATION

Introduction: Introduce the story and character. State your "thesis," which is a simple statement of your analysis of the character.

Body: Choose two characteristics, and give two or three examples from the story that show them.

Conclusion: Summarize your thesis. Add your opinion of the character and his or her importance in the story.

2. PRESENTATION CARDS

Write the outline for your presentation on index cards. Write large letters, leaving lots of space so it is easy for you to glance at while you are speaking. Mark the main points by highlighting or underlining. Remember that you will *not* be reading your cards during your presentation – you'll be using them only as a guide.

Example:

Student's Name:

Title: Maud in "Sadie and Maud" by Gwendolyn Brooks

| Introduction: | Maud, although she is an obedient and conservative daughter, grows up to be lonely and unhappy. |

Body:

1. Obedient – to society and parents, goes to college, lives in the old family house

2. Conservative – shares her parents' judgement/shame about Sadie's pregnancy

3. Unhappy – thin, brown mouse, alone, old house

Conclusion: She does everything that is expected of her, but loses her own happiness. The poet wants us to compare Maud with Sadie, who was unsuccessful in the usual sense, but happy and free.

Discussion Questions: Write at least four discussion questions which will stimulate your group members to share their opinions and experiences with each other.

Example:

> **DISCUSSION QUESTIONS:**
>
> 1. Have you ever been judged by your parents or friends for not following the expected rules? Describe your experience.
>
> 2. Who do you admire most, Sadie or Maud? Why?
>
> 3. If you were a parent, which type of child would you prefer, Sadie or Maud? Why?
>
> 4. In your opinion, which gives the best education: college or life experience? What seems to be the poet's opinion?

3. PRACTICING YOUR PRESENTATION

Practice with a tape recorder, using your notecards for reference (remember, don't read). Listen to the tape and notice the timing (5 to 8 minutes), volume, organization, etc. Tape yourself a few times. Your teacher may include the tape as part of your evaluation.

4. DURING THE SMALL-GROUP PRESENTATION

Be prepared, with good notecards.

Keep eye contact with the group.

Speak loudly.

Watch time.

During discussion, involve everyone.

Note: Even when you are not presenting, you have a big responsibility to participate in the other group members' discussion. Listen, encourage, respond, discuss.

III. Summary Paragraph

Summarize your main points from the small-group presentation in a paragraph. Remember to include a topic sentence, supporting examples, and a concluding sentence. Use your index cards as an outline.

IV. Suggested Essay Topics.

1. "Some of the stories and poem of this unit show the legacy which parents pass on to their children, emotionally, socially, and physically. This legacy is sometimes positive, and sometimes negative, but it is always inescapable." Discuss.

2. "Our world view as adults is shaped irrevocably by our childhood conflicts with our parents." Write a cause-and-effect essay responding to this statement.

3. "Like father, like son." Do the children of these stories mirror their parents' personalities?

UNIT 3

MEN & WOMEN

▲▲▲▲▲

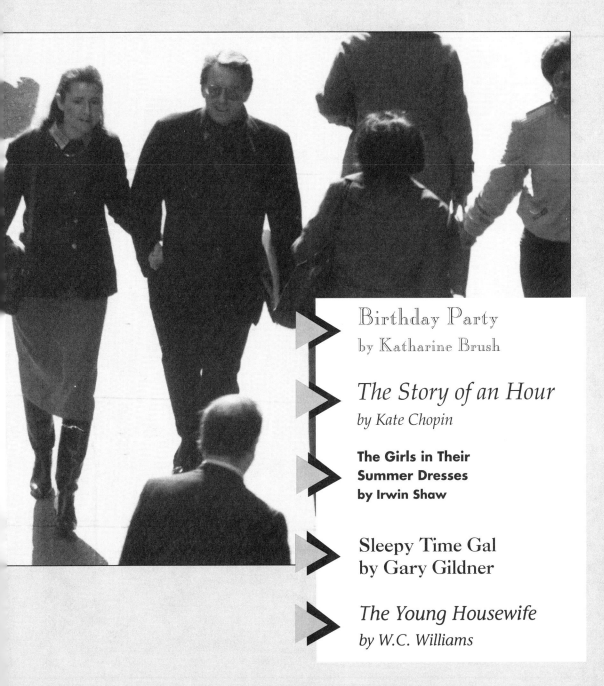

Birthday Party

by Katharine Brush

> *"...It suddenly became obvious that this was an Occasion — in fact, the husband's birthday, and the wife had planned a little surprise for him."*

Background:

In three short paragraphs, the author succeeds in creating a situation so realistic that the readers feel that they are in the restaurant observing this "party." The inside life of a marriage is revealed in a few embarrassing minutes.

Warm-up discussion/Response Journal:

1. What does the title, *Birthday Party* make you think of?

2. Why do most people like birthday parties? Why might someone not like to have a party for his or her birthday? Do you know anyone like that?

3. Have you ever sat in a restaurant and listened secretly to the other customers as they had conversations with each other? This is called "eavesdropping." Do you think it's fun or rude?

Guiding questions:

Read the story once quickly without using a dictionary. It is not necessary that you understand every word. Just concentrate on understanding the main ideas of the story.

1. *Who* are the main characters? What do you know about them

2. *Where* does the story take place?

3. *When* does the story take place?

4. *What* happens?

5. *What changes* occur in the story?

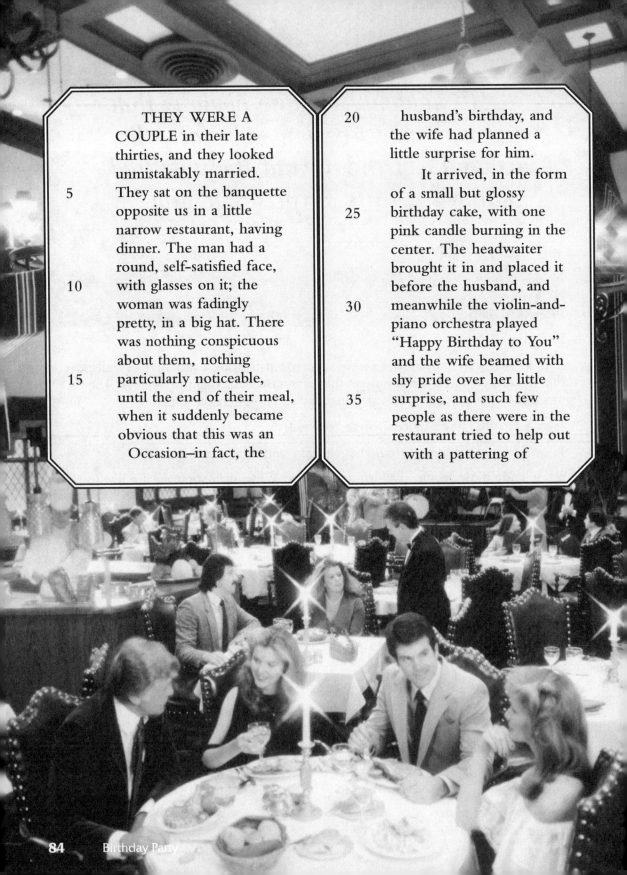

THEY WERE A COUPLE in their late thirties, and they looked unmistakably married.
5 They sat on the banquette opposite us in a little narrow restaurant, having dinner. The man had a round, self-satisfied face, with glasses on it; the
10 woman was fadingly pretty, in a big hat. There was nothing conspicuous about them, nothing particularly noticeable,
15 until the end of their meal, when it suddenly became obvious that this was an Occasion—in fact, the

20 husband's birthday, and the wife had planned a little surprise for him.

It arrived, in the form of a small but glossy
25 birthday cake, with one pink candle burning in the center. The headwaiter brought it in and placed it before the husband, and
30 meanwhile the violin-and-piano orchestra played "Happy Birthday to You" and the wife beamed with shy pride over her little
35 surprise, and such few people as there were in the restaurant tried to help out with a pattering of

applause. It became
40 clear at once that help was
needed, because the
husband was not pleased.
Instead he was hotly
embarrassed, and indignant
45 at his wife for
embarrassing him.

You looked at him
and you saw this and you
thought, "Oh, now, don't
50 *be* like that!" But he was
like that, and as soon as
the little cake had been
deposited on the table, and
the orchestra had finished
55 the birthday piece, and the
general attention had

shifted from the man
and the woman, I saw him
say something to her
60 under his breath—some
punishing thing, quick and
curt and unkind. I couldn't
bear to look at the woman
then, so I stared at my
65 plate and waited for quite
a long time. Not long
enough, though. She was
still crying when I finally
glanced over there again.
70 Crying quietly and heart-
brokenly and hopelessly,
all to herself, under the
gay big brim of her
best hat.

Birthday Party

Glossary

unmistakably	certainly, without question
banquette	a long bench placed against the wall
to fade	to lose strength or color
conspicuous	obvious, remarkable
glossy	shiny
to beam	to shine
a pattering	a light, quick sound (as the soft sound of rain)
indignant	angry (because of one's loss of pride or dignity)
curt	sharp
brim	the outer edge (for example, of a hat)

Comprehension and Interpretation

A. In this exercise, the first statement (a) is factual and the second statement (b) is inferential.

For (a), write true or false. For (b), write true or false, and the detail from the text which implies the answer.

_____ 1. a. The couple were probably about 25 years old.

_____   b. They had been married for a long time.

_____ 2. a. The restaurant was small and narrow.

_____   b. It was probably expensive.

_____ 3. a. The story is written in third person narration.

_____   b. The narrator is unsympathetic to the wife.

_____ 4. a. The husband was embarrassed and angry.

_____   b. He is probably a shy, proud man.

B. 1. What is the main conflict of the story, and the climax that develops from this conflict?

   2. Do you think the wife knows her husband dislikes birthday parties? If she doesn't know, what does that say about their relationship? If she does know, why did she plan the party anyway?

   3. What does the hat symbolize?

   4. How is the last sentence ironic?

Evaluation

Rank the following sentences according to how well you think they express the *theme* (for example, "1" means very well; "5" means not so well). Then compare your choices with your partner's.

___4___ Men are selfish.

___4___ It is wrong to embarrass someone in a public place.

___5___ Humans are selfish.

___1___ To understand one another is very difficult.

___1___ Failed communication in a marriage, though common, is tragic.

___1___ Our attempts at understanding and communication often fail.

___4___ Women are usually hurt by men.

If you can think of another theme of the story, write it here:

_____

_____

_____

Evaluation: Discussion or Response Journal

Does the narrator sympathize with the husband or the wife? How do you know? Who do you sympathize with? Why?

The Story of an Hour

by Kate Chopin

"She breathed a quick prayer that life might be long. It was only yesterday she had thought with a shudder that life might be long."

Background:

The irony of this short story, written about 100 years ago, still pleases modern readers. Most of the "action" occurs in the mind of Mrs. Mallard, and things change in a matter of minutes. Our assumptions about love and marriage are manipulated, resulting in a very surprising ending.

Warm-up Discussion/Response Journal:

1. Listen as your teacher reads the first paragraph of the story. In groups, make up your own ending which would complete the story. Tell your story to the class.

2. What kind of assumptions about marriage are expressed in your story? What is your general attitude to marriage? What do you consider the purpose, the advantages, and the disadvantages?

Guiding Questions:

Read the story once quickly without using a dictionary. It is not necessary that you understand every word. Just concentrate on understanding the main ideas of the story

1. **Who** are the main characters? What do you know about them?

2. **Where** does the story take place?

3. **When** does the story take place?

4. **What** happens?

5. **What changes** occur in the story?

KNOWING THAT MRS. MALLARD was afflicted with a heart trouble, great care was taken to break to her as gently as possible the news of her husband's death.

It was her sister Josephine who told her, in broken
5   sentences; veiled hints that revealed in half concealing. Her husband's friend Richards was there, too, near her. It was he who had been in the newspaper office when intelligence of the railroad disaster was received, with Brently Mallard's name leading the list of "killed." He
10 had only taken the time to assure himself of its truth by a second telegram, and had hastened to forestall any less careful, less tender friend in bearing the sad message.

She did not hear the story as many women have heard the same, with a paralyzed inability to accept its
15 significance. She wept at once, with sudden, wild abandonment, in her sister's arms. When the storm of grief had spent itself she went away to her room alone. She would have no one follow her.

There stood, facing the open window, a comfortable,
20 roomy armchair. Into this she sank, pressed down by a physical exhaustion that haunted her body and seemed to reach into her soul.

She could see in the open square before her house the tops of trees that were all aquiver with the new spring
25 life. The delicious breath of rain was in the air. In the street below a peddler was crying his wares. The notes of a distant song which some one was singing reached her faintly, and countless sparrows were twittering in the eaves.

30   There were patches of blue sky showing here and there through the clouds that had met and piled one above the other in the west facing her window.

She sat with her head thrown back upon the cushion of the chair, quite motionless, except when a sob came
35   up into her throat and shook her, as a child who has cried itself to sleep continues to sob in its dreams.

She was young, with a fair, calm face, whose lines bespoke repression and even a certain strength. But now there was a dull stare in her eyes, whose gaze was fixed
40   away off yonder on one of those patches of blue sky. It was not a glance of reflection, but rather indicated a suspension of intelligent thought.

There was something coming to her and she was waiting for it, fearfully. What was it? She did not know;
45   it was too subtle and elusive to name. But she felt it, creeping out of the sky, reaching toward her through the sounds, the scents, the color that filled the air.

Now her bosom rose and fell tumultuously. She was beginning to recognize this thing that was approaching to
50   possess her, and she was striving to beat it back with her will—as powerless as her two white slender hands would have been.

When she abandoned herself a little whispered word escaped her slightly parted lips. She said it over and over
55   under her breath: "free, free, free!" The vacant stare and the look of terror that had followed it went from her eyes. They stayed keen and bright. Her pulses beat fast, and the coursing blood warmed and relaxed every inch

of her body.

60   She did not stop to ask if it were or were not a
monstrous joy that held her. A clear and exalted
perception enabled her to dismiss the suggestion as
trivial.

She knew that she would weep again when she saw
65   the kind, tender hands folded in death; the face that had
never looked save with love upon her, fixed and gray and
dead. But she saw beyond that bitter moment a long
procession of years to come that would belong to her
absolutely. And she opened and spread her arms out to
70   them in welcome.

There would be no one to live for her during those
coming years; she would live for herself. There would be
no powerful will bending hers in that blind persistence
with which men and women believe they have a right to
75   impose a private will upon a fellow-creature. A kind
intention or a cruel intention made the act seem no less a
crime as she looked upon it in that brief moment of
illumination.

And yet she had loved him–sometimes. Often she had
80   not. What did it matter! What could love, the unsolved
mystery, count for in face of this possession of self-
assertion which she suddenly recognized as the strongest
impulse of her being!

"Free! Body and soul free!" she kept whispering.

85   Josephine was kneeling before the closed door with
her lips to the keyhole, imploring for admission. "Louise,

open the door! I beg; open the door—you will make yourself ill. What are you doing, Louise? For heaven's sake open the door."

90   "Go away. I am not making myself ill." No; she was drinking in a very elixir of life through that open window.

Her fancy was running riot along those days ahead of her. Spring days, and summer days, and all sorts of days

95   that would be her own. She breathed a quick prayer that life might be long. It was only yesterday she had thought with a shudder that life might be long.

She rose at length and opened the door to her sister's importunities. There was a feverish triumph in her eyes,

100   and she carried herself unwittingly like a goddess of Victory. She clasped her sister's waist, and together they descended the stairs. Richards stood waiting for them at the bottom.

Some one was opening the front door with a latchkey.

105   It was Brently Mallard who entered, a little travel-stained, composedly carrying his grip-sack and umbrella. He had been far from the scene of the accident, and did not even know there had been one. He stood amazed at Josephine's piercing cry; at Richards' quick motion to

110   screen him from the view of his wife.

But Richards was too late.

When the doctors came they said she had died of heart disease—of joy that kills.

The Story of an Hour

Glossary

veiled	hidden, not completely clear
intelligence	information, news
to hasten	to hurry
to forestall	to prevent
to abandon	to give oneself up to a strong emotion
to cry one's wares	to advertise what one is selling by shouting
to sob	to cry very hard
repression	to keep one's emotions hidden
subtle	very small and difficult to see or analyze
to exalt	to raise to a high position
trivial	not important
persistent	not giving up, stubborn
to impose	to force
elixir of life	a magic medicine which cures all sickness
"to run riot" (idiom)	to move wildly and freely
to shudder	to shiver (in fear or revulsion)
importunity	persistent request
unwittingly	unknowingly

Vocabulary in Context

Complete the following exercise by guessing a word for each blank . Don't check the text, but just choose any word that is logical and of the correct word form. Try to think of the most probable word.

1. Mrs. Mallard was ___afflicted___ with heart trouble.
2. (Richards) had only taken the time to ___assure___ himself of the (newspaper's) truth.
3. Countless sparrows were ___twittering___ in the eaves.
4. (Her dull stare) indicated a ___suspens___ of intelligent thought.
5. Men and women believe they have a right to ___impose___ their private will upon (each other)
6. Josephine was kneeling before the door, ___imploring___ for admission.

After you have finished, look at the story and scan for the above sentences in order to find the word which the author used. Write the words below, with their dictionary meaning. Were your guesses from context related in meaning to the words which the author used?

1. page 92 _____
2. page 92 _____
3. page 92 _____
4. page 93 _____
5. page 94 _____
6. page 94 _____

Comprehension Check

Read the story a second time, and answer the following True or False questions:

___T___ 1. Mrs. Louise Mallard has heart trouble.
___F___ 2. She reads about her husband, Mr. Brentley Mallard's, death in a newspaper.
___T___ 3. Her sister, Josephine, discusses the bad news gently because she is afraid to upset Mrs. Mallard.
___F___ 4. When Mrs. Mallard first hears the bad news, she doesn't cry at all.
___T___ 5. She goes to her room alone.
___F___ 6. The season is autumn.
___F___ 7. She is middle-aged.
___T___ 8. She is struck with a great sense of freedom.
___F___ 9. She prays for long life.
___F___ 10. The ghost of her husband, Mr. Brently Mallard, enters the house.
___T___ 11. When Mrs. Mallard sees him, she dies of a heart attack.

Response Check

As Mrs. Mallard thinks about her husband's death, she starts to feel joyful. Can you sympathize with her feeling? What do you think about her? Is she strange, a bad wife, crazy with grief, or just normal?

Comprehension: Summary

Fill in the blanks to complete the summary. If the blank begins with an initial, you must use a word beginning with that letter (found in the story).

Newspapers reported that _____ had died in a train _____.
As Mrs. Mallard was   a_____ with _____ trouble, great
care was taken to b_____ the news to her gently. At first she was filled with
g_____ but later, with j_____ because at last she would be
_____ . However, her husband really _____ died, and when
Mrs. Mallard saw him walk in the front door, she _____.

Word Study: Synonyms

Match the following words with the appropriate synonyms in the story:

1.   (page 92, paragraph 1) to have trouble with   _____

2.   (92; 3)   cried   _____

3.   (92; 3)   sorrow   _____

4.   (92; 5)   singing   _____

5.   (93; 5)   stormily   _____

6.   (93; 6)   empty   _____

7.   (93; 6)   fear   _____

8.   (95; 3)   shiver   _____

9.   (95; 4)   held   _____

Most of these synonyms have a slightly difference nuance. Use your dictionary to find the shared meaning and the different nuance.

1. *afflicted–caused pain or suffering*

2.

3.

4.

5.

6.

7.

8.

9.

Interpretation

1. How much time passes in this story?

2. Describe Mrs. Mallard's changing emotions by putting the following in correct order: grief/ joy/ fear/ relaxation/ emptiness/ anticipation/ grief

3. How does the scene from her window apparently contrast with her emotional state? How does this apparent contrast change?

4. Re-read page 93, lines 43 to 52. What is the "something" that Mrs. Mallard senses coming toward her?

5. Re-read page 94, lines 71 to 98. What is meant by "crime"? Whose crime?

6. What kind of husband was Mr. Mallard? How do you know?

7. Did Mrs. Mallard love her husband? How do you know?

8. Account for Mrs. Mallard's joy.

9. What sentence from the story best represents the change in Mrs. Mallard's attitude to life? What sentence best represents the change in her attitude to herself?

10. This story is doubly ironic.

   a. How might the tragedy be ironic for the characters in the story (Mr. Richards, Josephine)?

   b. How is the story ironic for the reader? (Look at the last sentence.)

Evaluation: Discussion or Response Journal

Summarize the attitude to marriage that this story presents. Do you agree or disagree?

The Girls in their Summer Dresses

by Irwin Shaw

"You always look at other women," Francis said. "Everywhere. Every damned place we go."

Background:

The difficulty of communication and understanding between husband and wife is shown in the dialogue which forms the basis of this story. In the end, the communication that is achieved leaves only unhappiness and no apparent possibility of change. As you read the story, notice which character you are sympathizing with, and why.

Warm-up Discussion:

Decide if you agree or disagree with the following statements. Then choose the three statements that you agree with most strongly, and compare them with a classmate's.

a. It's okay for a married man to flirt with other women, but he should never have an affair (sexual relationship) with them.
b. If a marriage partner has an affair, the husband or wife should ignore it forgivingly.
c. It is okay for a married woman to have affairs with other men.
d. Women are more faithful than men.
e. For men to "watch women" is natural, and can't be helped.

Read the story once quickly without using a dictionary. It is not necessary that you understand every word. Just concentrate on understanding the main ideas of the story.

1. **Who** are the main characters? What do you know about them?

2. **Where** does the story take place?

3. **When** does the story take place?

4. **What** happens?

5. **What changes** occur in the story? Why?

FIFTH AVENUE WAS SHINING in the sun when they left the Brevoort. The sun was warm, even though it was February, and everything looked like Sunday morning–the buses and the well-dressed people walking slowly in couples and the quiet buildings with the windows closed.

Michael held Frances' arm tightly as they walked toward Washington Square in the sunlight. They walked lightly, almost smiling, because they had slept late and had a good breakfast and it was Sunday. Michael unbuttoned his coat and let it flap around him in the mild wind.

"Look out," Frances said as they crossed Eighth Street. "You'll break your neck."

Michael laughed and Frances laughed with him.

"She's not so pretty," Frances said. "Anyway, not pretty enough to take a chance of breaking your neck."

Michael laughed again. "How did you know I was looking at her?"

Frances cocked her head to one side and smiled at her husband under the brim of her hat. "Mike, darling," she said.

"O.K.," he said. "Excuse me."

Frances patted his arm lightly and pulled him along a little faster toward Washington Square. "Let's not see anybody all day," she said. "Let's just hang around with each other. You and me. We're always up to our neck in people, drinking their Scotch or drinking our Scotch; we only see each other in bed. I want to go out with my husband all day long. I want him to talk only to me and listen only to me."

"What's to stop us?" Michael asked.

"The Stevensons. They want us to drop by around one

o'clock and they'll drive us into the country."

"The cunning Stevensons," Mike said. "Transparent. They can whistle. They can go driving in the country by

35 themselves."

"Is it a date?"

"It's a date."

Frances leaned over and kissed him on the tip of the ear.

"Darling," Michael said, "this is Fifth Avenue."

40 "Let me arrange a program," Frances said. "A planned Sunday in New York for a young couple with money to throw away."

"Go easy."

"First let's go to the Metropolitan Museum of Art,"

45 Frances suggested, because Michael had said during the week he wanted to go. "I haven't been there in three years and there're at least ten pictures I want to see again. Then we can take the bus down to Radio City and watch them skate. And later we'll go down to Cavanaugh's and get a

50 steak as big as a blacksmith's apron, with a bottle of wine, and after that there's a French picture at the Filmarte that everybody says—say, are you listening to me?"

"Sure," he said. He took his eyes off the hatless girl with the dark hair, cut dancer-style like a helmet, who was

55 walking past him.

"That's the program for the day," Frances said flatly. "Or maybe you'd just rather walk up and down Fifth Avenue."

"No," Michael said. "Not at all."

"You always look at other women," Frances said.

60 "Everywhere. Every damned place we go."

"No, darling," Michael said, "I look at everything. God gave me eyes and I look at women and men and subway excavations and moving pictures and the little flowers of the field. I casually inspect the universe."

65   "You ought to see the look in your eye," Frances said, "as you casually inspect the universe on Fifth Avenue."

    "I'm a happily married man." Michael pressed her elbow tenderly. "Example for the whole twentieth century—Mr. and Mrs. Mike Loomis. Hey, let's have a drink," he said,
70   stopping.

    "We just had breakfast."

    "Now listen, darling," Mike said, choosing his words with care, "it's a nice day and we both felt good and there's no reason why we have to break it up. Let's have a nice
75   Sunday."

    "All right. I don't know why I started this. Let's drop it. Let's have a good time."

    They joined hands consciously and walked without talking among the baby carriages and the old Italian men in
80   their Sunday clothes and the young women with Scotties in Washington Square Park.

    "At least once a year everyone should go to the Metropolitan Museum of Art," Frances said after a while, her tone a good imitation of the tone she had used at
85   breakfast and at the beginning of their walk. "And it's nice on Sunday. There're a lot of people looking at the pictures and you get the feeling maybe Art isn't on the decline in New York City, after all—"

    "I want to tell you something," Michael said very
90   seriously. "I have not touched another woman. Not once. In all the five years."

    "All right," Frances said.

    "You believe that, don't you?"

"All right."

95   They walked between the crowded benches, under the scrubby city-park trees.

"I try not to notice it," Frances said, "but I feel rotten inside, in my stomach, when we pass a woman and you look at her and I see that look in your eye and that's the way you 100 looked at me the first time. In Alice Maxwell's house. Standing there in the living room, next to the radio, with a green hat on and all those people."

"I remember the hat," Michael said.

"The same look," Frances said. "And it makes me feel bad. 105 It makes me feel terrible."

"Sh-h-h, please, darling, sh-h-h."

"I think I would like a drink now," Frances said.

They walked over to a bar on Eighth Street, not saying anything. Michael automatically helping her over curbstones 110 and guiding her past automobiles. They sat near a window in the bar and the sun streamed in and there was a small, cheerful fire in the fireplace. A little Japanese waiter came over and put down some pretzels and smiled happily at them.

"What do you order after breakfast?" Michael asked.

115   "Brandy, I suppose," Frances said.

"Courvoisier," Michael told the waiter. "Two Courvoisiers."

The waiter came with the glasses and they sat drinking the brandy in the sunlight. Michael finished half his and drank a 120 little water.

"I look at women," he said. "Correct. I don't say it's wrong or right. I look at them. If I pass them on the street and I don't look at them, I'm fooling you, I'm fooling myself."

"It's not the fur coats. Or the hats. That's just the scenery for that particular kind of woman. Understand," he said, "you don't have to listen to this."

"I want to listen."

160 "I like the girls in the offices. Neat, with their eyeglasses, smart, chipper, knowing what everything is about. I like the girls on Forty-fourth Street at lunchtime, the actresses, all dressed up on nothing a week. I like the salesgirls in the stores, paying attention to you first because you're a man,

165 leaving lady customers waiting. I got all this stuff accumulated in me because I've been thinking about it for ten years and now you've asked for it and here it is."

"Go ahead," Frances said.

"When I think of New York City, I think of all the girls

170 on parade in the city. I don't know whether it's something special with me or whether every man in the city walks around with the same feeling inside him, but I feel as though I'm at a picnic in this city. I like to sit near the women in the theatres, the famous beauties who've taken

175 six hours to get ready and look it. And the young girls at the football games, with the red cheeks, and when the warm weather comes, the girls in their summer dresses." He finished his drink. "That's the story."

Frances finished her drink and swallowed two or three

180 times extra. "You say you love me?"

"I love you."

"I'm pretty, too," Frances said. "As pretty as any of them."

"You're beautiful," Michael said.

185 "I'm good for you," Frances said, pleading. "I've made a good wife, a good housekeeper, a good friend. I'd do any

damn thing for you."

"I know," Michael said. He put his hand out and grasped hers.

190   "You'd like to be free to–" Frances said.

"Sh-h-h."

"Tell the truth." She took her hand away from under his.

Michael flicked the edge of his glass with his finger. "O.K.," he said gently. "Sometimes I feel I would like to be

195   free."

"Well," Frances said, "any time you say."

"Don't be foolish." Michael swung his chair around to her side of the table and patted her thigh.

She began to cry silently into her handkerchief, bent over

200   just enough so that nobody else in the bar would notice. "Someday," she said, crying, "you're going to make a move."

Michael didn't say anything. He sat watching the bartender slowly peel a lemon.

205   "Aren't you?" Frances asked harshly. "Come on, tell me. Talk. Aren't you?"

"Maybe," Michael said. He moved his chair back again. "How the hell do I know?"

"You know," Frances persisted. "Don't you know?"

210   "Yes," Michael said after a while, "I know."

Frances stopped crying then. Two or three snuffles into the handkerchief and she put it away and her face didn't tell anything to anybody. "At least do me one favor," she said.

"Sure."

215   "Stop talking about how pretty this woman is or that one. Nice eyes, nice breasts, a pretty figure, good voice." She

mimicked his voice. "Keep it to yourself. I'm not interested."

Michael waved to the waiter. "I'll keep it to myself," he said.

Frances flicked the corners of her eyes. "Another brandy," she told the waiter.

"Two," Michael said.

"Yes, Ma'am, yes sir," said the waiter, backing away.

Frances regarded Michael coolly across the table. "Do you want me to call the Stevensons?" she asked. "It'll be nice in the country."

"Sure," Michael said. "Call them."

She got up from the table and walked across the room toward the telephone. Michael watched her walk, thinking what a pretty girl, what nice legs.

The Girls in their Summer Dresses

Glossary

"break your neck" (idiom)	hurt yourself; have an accident
to cock	to turn, move, or raise attentively or knowingly
brim	the edge (of a hat or a cup, for example)
up to our necks in (idiom)	too much of, a lot of
"they can whistle" (idiom)	they can do anything, but we will do as we please
"with money to throw away"	rich
"go easy"	be careful
Scotties	Scotch terrier (dog)
chipper	fresh, cheerful
"any time you say"	go ahead
"make a move"	sexually approach a woman
harshly	strongly, severely
to mimic	to copy or imitate (usually to make fun of)

Comprehension Check

Read the story a second time, trying to find answers to the following questions:

1. Describe the setting.
2. What is Frances wearing?
3. Why does Mike apologize?
4. What does Frances suggest they do? Why?
5. Where did Mike see Frances the first time? What was she wearing?
6. Michael classifies the women he likes to look at into seven groups. What are they?
7. "Someday," she said, crying, "you're going to make a move." Does Michael deny Frances' accusations?
8. What favor does Frances ask of Michael?
9. What does Michael notice as Frances walks across the room?

Comprehension Check: Summary

On a beautiful _____ morning, Frances and Michael had planned to
_____ , but Frances suggests that they _____ a romantic day alone
together instead. Mike _____ , but soon they get into an _____
because of his habit of always _____ attractive women. In a bar, he
_____ that he loves watching _____ and that in the future he will
probably _____ . Frances is _____ but Mike _____ change.
In the end, they do not spend the day alone, but instead, _____ .

Response Check

Do you sympathize with Michael, or Frances, or both? What should they do?

Interpretation I: A Closer Look at Language

Make a list of the verbs, adjectives, and adverbs in the first two paragraphs. What
conflicting moods are set up? How does the scene reflect Frances and Michael's
relationship? What can you deduce about Michael's character?

Interpretation II

A. Choose the best answer for each of the following statements about the story.

1. Frances suggests that they go to the Metropolitan Museum of Art because
    a. she's wanted to go there for a long time.
    b. it's a good way to spend free time.
    c. Michael wants to go there.

2. Michael likes the salesgirls in the stores because
    a. they're very pretty.
    b. they serve him before they serve the women customers.
    c. they wear beautiful summer dresses.

3. Why does the expression in Mike's eye as he looks at a passing girl bother Frances?
    a. She realizes he views strange women in the same way that he views her.
    b. She's afraid he likes them better than her.
    c. He ignores her.

4. The last line tells us that
   a. Michael will always love his wife the most.
   b. Michael will continue to view her as he views all women.
   c. Frances should be pleased to be admired by Michael.

5. The conclusion of their brief honest communication is
   a. Frances will ignore Michael's behavior in the future.
   b. Michael will try his best to change.
   c. Frances realizes she was being selfish to complain.

Evaluation: Discussion or Response Journal

1. Is Michael's girl-watching a serious offence?
2. Is the unhappiness at the end of the story inevitable?
3. If you were Frances, what would you do? If you were Michael, what would you do?

Interpretation III

Read the following quotation taken from a book called *Ways of Seeing* by John Berger:

"Men survey women before treating them. Consequently how a woman appears to a man can determine how she will be treated. . .One might simplify this by saying: men act and women appear. Men look at women. Women watch themselves being looked at. This determines not only most relations between men and women, but also the relation of women to themselves. The surveyor of woman in herself is male: the surveyed female. Thus she turns herself into an object - and most particularly an object of vision: a sight."

1. Relate Berger's statement to the following exchange between Frances and Michael. What does Michael remember about their first meeting? What does Frances remember?

"I try not to notice it," Frances said, "but I feel rotten inside, in my stomach, when we pass a woman and you look at her and I see that look in your eye and that's the way you looked at me the first time. In Alice Maxwell's house. Standing there in the living room, next to the radio, with a green hat on and all those people." "I remember the hat," Michael said. "The same look," Frances said.

2. What is the symbolic significance of hats in the story?
3. Do women encourage men to see them as "objects"?
4. In your opinion, does this story describe a conflict of individual desire, or an inevitable incompatibility between men and women?

Small-Group Debate

Debating question: "Michael should stop his girl-watching."

Sit in groups of two or three. Your teacher will assign your group the "pro" (agree with debating question) or "con" (disagree with debating question) side. When you are ready to begin, you will be debating against another small group, so there will be several debates happening at the same time. The following is a suggested time sequence:

1. Preparing arguments – 15 minutes. You should write down the arguments which support your position in note form.
2. Presentation of main arguments – 5 minutes Side A, 5 minutes Side B
3. Planning the rebuttal – 10 minutes
4. Presentation of rebuttal – 3 minutes Side A, 3 minutes Side B
5. Planning final statements and summaries – 4 minutes
6. Presentation of final arguments – 2 minutes Side A, 2 minutes Side B

Evaluation: Discussion or Response Journal

1. The situation in the story seems to reflect John Berger's ideas about "women as sex objects." If indeed "men look at women; women watch themselves being looked at," is this a bad situation? Can you find examples from advertising, adult cartoons, magazines or music which show women as sex objects?
2. Describe the characters' attitudes to marriage. How do their attitudes compare to yours?

Sleepy Time Gal

by Gary Gildner

"It was my mother who said the girl would rest her head on Phil's shoulder while he played, and that he got the idea for the song from the pretty way she looked when she got sleepy."

Background:

The nostalgia evoked by this old-fashioned love story will please most readers. But perhaps more interesting than the simple love story itself is the complex manner of storytelling. The narrator, his father, and his mother each try to tell the same story, but with important differences.

Warm-up Discussion/Response Journal:

1. What do you know about the "Depression" in the United States? Do you know anyone who lived at that time? Have you heard their stories about the difficulties of daily life?

2. In your point of view, is it better to marry for money or for love? Should people of different social class marry each other? Is your opinion similar to the general thinking of your culture?

3. Have you ever been told the same story by two different people and realized that the stories were quite different? Why do you suppose this happens? Are people so dishonest that they knowingly change "what really happened" when they tell someone else about it?

Guiding Questions:

Read the story once quickly without using a dictionary. It is not necessary that you understand every word. Just concentrate on getting the main ideas.

1. **Who** are the main characters? What do you know about them?

2. **Where** does the story take place?

3. **When** does the story take place?

4. **What** happens?

5. **What changes** occur in the story? Why?

125   "You look at them as though you want them," Frances
said, playing with her brandy glass. "Every one of them."

       "In a way," Michael said, speaking softly and not to his
wife, "in a way that's true. I don't do anything about it, but
it's true."

130   "I know it. That's why I feel bad."

       "Another brandy," Michael called. "Waiter, two more
brandies."

       He sighed and closed his eyes and rubbed them gently
with his fingertips. "I love the way women look. One of the
135   things I like best about New York is the battalions of
women. When I first came to New York from Ohio that
was the first thing I noticed, the million wonderful women,
all over the city. I walked around with my heart in my
throat."

140   "A kid," Frances said. "That's a kid's feeling."

       "Guess again," Michael said. "Guess again. I'm older
now. I'm a man getting near middle age, putting on a little
fat and I still love to walk along Fifth Avenue at three
o'clock on the east side of the street between Fiftieth and
145   Fifty-seventh Streets. They're all out then, shopping, in their
furs and their crazy hats, everything all concentrated from
all over the world into seven blocks—the best furs, the best
clothes, the handsomest women, out to spend money and
feeling good about it."

150   The Japanese waiter put the two drinks down, smiling
with great happiness.

       "Everything is all right?" he asked.

       "Everything is wonderful," Michael said.

       "If it's just a couple of fur coats," Frances said, "and
155   forty-five-dollar hats... ."

IN THE SMALL TOWN in northern Michigan where my father lived as a young man, he had an Italian friend who worked in a restaurant. I will call his friend Phil. Phil's job in the restaurant was as ordinary as you can imagine—

5 from making coffee in the morning to sweeping up at night. But what was not ordinary about Phil was his piano playing. On Saturday nights my father and Phil and their girlfriends would drive ten or fifteen miles to a roadhouse by a lake where they would drink beer from schoopers and dance and

10 Phil would play an old beat-up piano. He could play any song you named, my father said, but the song everyone waited for was the one he wrote, which he would always play at the end before they left to go back to the town. And everyone knew of course that he had written the song for

15 his girl, who was as pretty as she was rich. Her father was the banker in their town, and he was a tough old German, and he didn't like Phil going around with his daughter.

My father, when he told the story, which was not often, would tell it in an offhand way and emphasize the

20 Depression and not having much, instead of the important parts. I will try to tell it the way he did, if I can.

So they would go to the roadhouse by the lake, and finally Phil would play his song, and everyone would say, Phil, that's a great song, you could make a lot of money

25 from it. But Phil would only shake his head and smile and look at his girl. I have to break in here and say that my father, a gentle but practical man, was not inclined to emphasize the part about Phil looking at his girl. It was my mother who said the girl would rest her head on Phil's

30 shoulder while he played, and that he got the idea for the song from the pretty way she looked when she got sleepy. My mother was not part of the story, but she had heard it

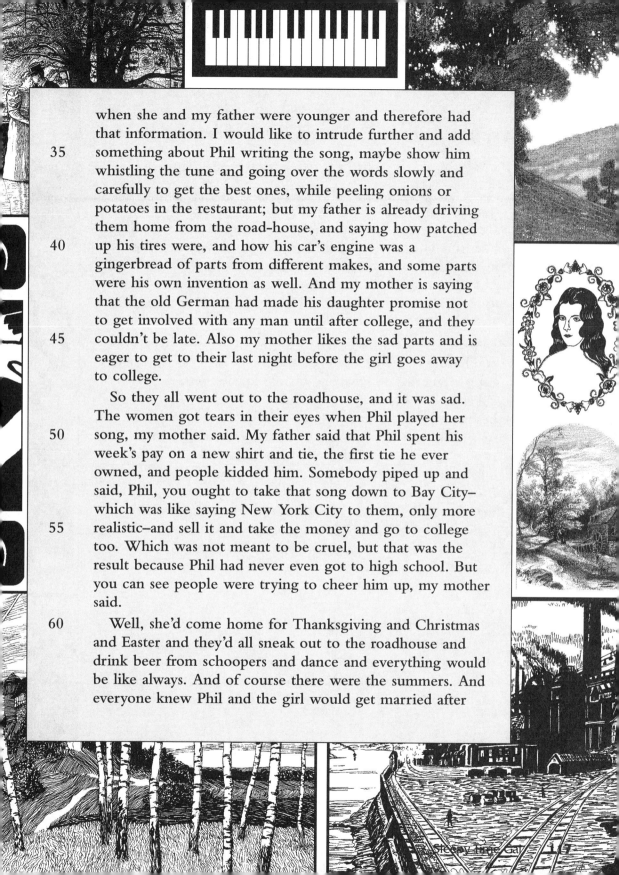

when she and my father were younger and therefore had
that information. I would like to intrude further and add
35 something about Phil writing the song, maybe show him
whistling the tune and going over the words slowly and
carefully to get the best ones, while peeling onions or
potatoes in the restaurant; but my father is already driving
them home from the road-house, and saying how patched
40 up his tires were, and how his car's engine was a
gingerbread of parts from different makes, and some parts
were his own invention as well. And my mother is saying
that the old German had made his daughter promise not
to get involved with any man until after college, and they
45 couldn't be late. Also my mother likes the sad parts and is
eager to get to their last night before the girl goes away
to college.

So they all went out to the roadhouse, and it was sad.
The women got tears in their eyes when Phil played her
50 song, my mother said. My father said that Phil spent his
week's pay on a new shirt and tie, the first tie he ever
owned, and people kidded him. Somebody piped up and
said, Phil, you ought to take that song down to Bay City—
which was like saying New York City to them, only more
55 realistic—and sell it and take the money and go to college
too. Which was not meant to be cruel, but that was the
result because Phil had never even got to high school. But
you can see people were trying to cheer him up, my mother
said.

60 Well, she'd come home for Thanksgiving and Christmas
and Easter and they'd all sneak out to the roadhouse and
drink beer from schoopers and dance and everything would
be like always. And of course there were the summers. And
everyone knew Phil and the girl would get married after

65 she made good her promise to her father because you could
see it in their eyes when he sat at the old beat-up piano and
played her song.

That last part about their eyes was not, of course, in my
father's telling, but I couldn't help putting it in there even
70 though I know it is making some of you impatient.
Remember that this happened many years ago in the woods
by a lake in northern Michigan, before television. I wish I
could put more in, especially about the song and how it felt
to Phil to sing it and how the girl felt when hearing it and
75 knowing it was hers, but I've already intruded too much in
a simple story that isn't even mine.

Well, here's the kicker part. Probably by now many of
you have guessed that one vacation near the end she doesn't
come home to see Phil, because she meets some guy at
80 college who is good-looking and as rich as she is and,
because her father knew about Phil all along and was
pressuring her into forgetting about him, she gives in to this
new guy and goes to his hometown during the vacation and
falls in love with him. That's how the people in town
85 figured it, because after she graduates they turn up, already
married, and right away he takes over the old German's
bank—and buys a new Pontiac at the place where my father
is the mechanic and pays cash for it. The paying cash always
made my father pause and shake his head and mention
90 again that times were tough, but here comes this guy in a
spiffy white shirt (with French cuffs, my mother said) and
pays the full price in cash.

And this made my father shake his head too: Phil took
the song down to Bay City and sold it for twenty-five
95 dollars, the only money he ever got for it. It was the same
song we'd just heard on the radio and which reminded my

father of the story I just told you. What happened to Phil?
Well, he stayed in Bay City and got a job managing a movie
theater. My father saw him there after the Depression when
100   he was on his way to Detroit to work for Ford. He stopped
and Phil gave him a box of popcorn. The song he wrote for
the girl has sold many millions of records, and if I told you
the name of it you could probably sing it, or at least whistle
the tune. I wonder what the girl thinks when she hears it.
105   Oh yes, my father met Phil's wife too. She worked in the
movie theater with him, selling tickets and cleaning the
carpet after the show with one of those sweepers you push.
She was also big and loud and nothing like the other one,
my mother said.

Sleepy Time Gal

Glossary

beat-up	in poor condition because of too much use
offhand	casual, without thought or preparation
the Depression	the bad economic times of the 1930's
to intrude	to go or join in without being invited or wanted
patched up	repaired with small pieces of material to cover the holes
"a gingerbread of parts" (idiom)	many different parts put together
to kid	to joke, to tease
to pipe up	to begin talking
to sneak out	to go out secretly
"the kicker part" (idiom)	the most important part
spiffy	fashionable, smart

Comprehension Check

A. True or False?

____ 1. The story takes place in a city in Ohio.

____ 2. The story takes place in the narrator's father's youth.

____ 3. Phil works in a gas station.

____ 4. Phil plays the piano on Saturday nights.

____ 5. Phil wrote a song for his girlfriend.

____ 6. The girlfriend's father doesn't like Phil.

____ 7. The main characters of the story are the narrator's father and mother.

____ 8. Phil and his girlfriend go to the same college.

____ 9. After the girl graduates, she marries a handsome, rich classmate.

____ 10. Phil's song becomes popular and he becomes rich.

B. Compare and contrast the following characters in terms of their job, education, wealth, and appearance.

	Phil	Phil's girlfriend	Phil's girlfriend's father	Phil's girlfriend's husband	Phil's wife
job					
education					
wealth					
appearance					

Comprehension and Interpretation

There are three people telling the story of "Sleepy Time Gal": the narrator, the father, and the mother. Identify who contributes the following information:

1. _____ Everyone loved the song Phil wrote for his girlfriend.
2. _____ Phil always looked at his girl while he played.
3. _____ He got the idea for the song from the pretty way his girlfriend looked when she got sleepy.
4. _____ Phil made up the song while peeling potatoes in the restaurant.
5. _____ Those years of the Depression were really hard times.
6. _____ The girlfriend's father made her promise not get involved with any man until after college.
7. _____ The last night before she went to college, Phil got dressed up.
8. _____ All the women cried when Phil played the song.
9. _____ When people saw the look in the couple's eyes, everyone knew they would get married.
10. _____ The girl's husband paid cash for his new Pontiac.
11. _____ Phil moved to Bay City and got a job in a movie theater.
12. _____ Phil's wife was big and loud.

Evaluation: Response Journal

1. Whose version of *Sleepy Time Gal* do you think is the closest to the truth? Say why you think so and why you think the other stories are inaccurate. Whose story do you like best? Why?

2. Rewrite the story, *Sleepy Time Gal* from the point of view of the girl (the banker's daughter) or someone who has heard the story from her. Try to keep the basic facts the same. This means that you'll need to determine which are the "true" facts of the story.

3. Rewrite the story from the seventh paragraph ("Well, here's the kicker part") so that it has a happy ending. Then explain if you think your new ending changes the themes of the story and how it changes them.

The Young Housewife

by William Carlos Williams

What are your associations with the following words? Brainstorm and list any adjectives, verbs, or nouns which come to your mind.

1. a young housewife

2. a car driver

3. a fallen leaf

Listen as your teacher reads the first stanza. Describe the wife. Who is "I"?

Listen as your teacher reads the second stanza. Describe the wife. How might she be like a "fallen leaf"?

Listen to the last stanza. How does the speaker feel? How do you feel?

The Young Housewife

At ten A.M. the young housewife
moves about in negligee behind
the wooden walls of her husband's house.
I pass solitary in my car.

Then again she comes to the curb
to call the ice-man, fish-man, and stands
shy, uncorseted, tucking in
stray ends of hair, and I compare her
to a fallen leaf.

The noiseless wheels of my car
rush with a crackling sound over
dried leaves as I bow and pass smiling.

William Carlos Williams

The Young Housewife

negligee	a woman's long, loose nightgown (pajama); usually pretty or "sexy"
solitary	alone
uncorseted	a corset is underwear worn to support and shape the waist and hips; "uncorseted" means not wearing a corset
to tuck in	to push behind or under securely
crackling	making dry, sharp, snapping noises

Comprehension and Interpretation

a. There are several comparisons and contrasts in this poem. Complete the following chart:

	wife	driver
similarity	she is inside a _____ alone	he is inside a car _____
difference	_____ house she is staying _____ she is being watched	"my" car he is _____ somewhere he is _____

b. Speaker and Tone

Who is speaking? Do you think he has ever watched the housewife before this morning? Why does he smile as he passes her?

The *tone* is the mood of the poem and is set by the attitude of the speaker. Is the tone of this poem: playful, light, serious, sarcastic, ironic, bitter, grim, violent, joyful, peaceful, ambivalent, sinister?

POETIC FEATURES: MUSICAL DEVICES

Onomatopoeia is the use of a word that imitates by its sound. For example, "crash!" or "crunch." What words can you find in the last stanza which are onomatopoeic? What is the effect of this musical device on the tone?

THEME

What is the driver's view of the housewife? Do you think this represents his general view towards women? What is the housewife's life situation and her attitude towards herself? What do you think the poet wants to show us?

CHORAL READING

In groups of three or four, prepare a "choral reading" of the poem. The choral reading is a dramatic reading, and the purpose is for your group to read the poem in such a way that its tone and meaning are clear to the audience.

When you read it as a group, you may have everyone read all of the lines together, or give certain people certain parts. Vary the volume, speed, and emphasis. When you are ready, perform it for the class.

UNIT 3 PROJECTS

I. Analysis of an Argumentative (Persuasive) Essay

Read the essay below and answer the questions which follow.

TITLE: IS MRS. JONG A GOOD MOTHER?

Every culture has its stereotypes of "the good mother." Loving, warm, forgiving, kind, and gentle describes the "mom" most children yearn for. Mrs. Jong, in "Rules of the Game" by Amy Tan, appears irritating, vain, and pushy. However, she is an effective parent for Waverly, and teaches her important lessons: self-discipline, self-confidence, and learning how to live "strategically" by following rules and weighing the consequences of one's actions.

In many ways, Mrs. Jong appears to be a "bad mother." Her unattractive characteristics can be seen from Amy Tan's choice of language–she "scolds" Waverly, she "twists and yanks" her hair, she has a "tight, proud smile," she gives advice to Waverly about playing chess even though she herself doesn't know the rules, she stands over Waverly as she tries to practice, and finally, she forces Waverly to walk with her in the market so that she can show off her famous daughter. All of these things irritate Waverly so much that she finally loses her temper, insults her mother, and runs away.

However, there is much to admire in Mrs. Jong's character, and she teaches her daughter important things by example and by her words. Waverly herself attributes her most important lesson to her mother's strict teaching: "I was six when my mother taught me the art of invisible strength. It was a strategy for winning arguments, respect from others, and eventually . . . chess games." Even so small an action as not crying for candy in the store is rewarded by Mrs. Jong. This self-discipline serves Waverly in her future chess games. Her mother also teaches her pride. Although Mrs. Jong cannot speak English fluently and cannot read it at all, she still maintains a pride in her heritage: "Chinese people do many things. Chinese people do business, do medicine, do painting. Not lazy like American people. We do torture. Best torture." She warns Waverly that it is very important to know the rules–of chess and of society – "Every time people come out from foreign country, must know rules. You not know, judge say, Too bad, go back. . . ."

Most importantly, Waverly learns that human relationships require great skill and strategy. She learns how to "win" in interactions with her mother. For example, instead of demanding to be allowed to play in local chess tournaments, she adopts a humble attitude, appropriate in her Chinese culture, and "bites back her tongue." Her mother then allows her to attend! Unfortunately, she can not control her temper in the market place, and hurts her mother's feelings deeply. As the story ends, Waverly is reflecting on the intricate "game" of her relationship with her mother, who is irritating and pushy, but also wise and loving.

Waverly's success as a chess player, and her wisdom in human relationships, even at an early age, can be attributed to the strong role model of her mother. Perhaps Mrs. Jong is too strict, too vain, too smug. However, she teaches Waverly how to survive in an often hostile society, with cleverness and respect.

1. Underline the thesis statement. Does the essay offer a "plan of development" in the introduction–that is, can you predict what the body paragraphs will deal with?

2. Underline the topic sentence of Body 1 paragraph. How does it relate to the introduction (draw an arrow)? What is the purpose of this paragraph? What examples does the writer give to support her opinion?

3. Underline the topic sentence of the Body 2 paragraph. How does it relate to the introduction (draw an arrow)? What examples does the writer give to support her opinion?

4. Underline the restatement of the thesis.

II. Essay topics: In an argumentative style essay, present your opinion on one of the following statements:

1. The poem, "The Young Housewife" and the short story *The Girls in their Summer Dresses* demonstrate the unequal power relations between men and women.

2. All the women in these four stories–*Birthday Party*, *The Story of an Hour*, *The Girls in their Summer Dresses*, and *Sleepytime Gal*–are selfish, vain, and unrealistic.

3. Explain what you think the basic conflicts and themes of *Sleepytime Gal* are, and how they relate to the general theme of "power and powerlessness" which underlies this textbook. Consider the power of social class, the power of love, and the power of storytelling. Shape your essay in an argumentative style of organization–you will need to form a "debatable" thesis statement which gives your opinion on an aspect of the story.

UNIT 4

Us
AND
THEM
▲▲▲▲▲

Sunday in the Park

by Bel Kaufman

"She sensed that it was more than just an unpleasant incident, more than defeat of reason by force."

Sunday in the Park by Bel Kaufman

So What Are You, Anyway? by Lawrence Hill

The following two "short-short" stories show conflict originating from social class and race. The characters in Story A, *Sunday in the Park*, use the threat of physical force to resolve the conflict, while the characters in Story B, *So What Are You, Anyway?* exert power through more subtle, psychological force. Half the class should read Story A and the other half Story B . In groups of four or five, students will analyze and discuss their story, and prepare to explain it to another group.

1. You might use the Guide to Reading Fiction (page 14-15) as a guide for your group's discussion about your story.

2. After your group is satisfied with its understanding of the story, prepare five key questions about the story - character, conflict, theme, etc.–which you think highlight the important issues. Write these out clearly.

3. Prepare a mime of the story, and then perform it for one of the groups that read the other story. The group that watches the mime must try to guess the plot.

4. After the mimes have been performed, read the story you saw mimed. Then sit with a student from the other group. Work on the questions together.

IT WAS STILL WARM in the late-afternoon sun, and the city noises came muffled through the trees in the park. She put her book down on the bench, removed her sunglasses, and sighed

5 contentedly. Morton was reading the *Times Magazine* section, one arm flung around her shoulder; their three-year-old son, Larry, was playing in the sandbox: a faint breeze fanned her hair softly against her cheek. It was five-thirty of a Sunday afternoon,

10 and the small playground, tucked away in a corner of the park, was all but deserted. The swings and seesaws stood motionless and abandoned, the slides were empty, and only in the sandbox two little boys squatted diligently side by side. *How good this is*, she

15 thought, and almost smiled at her sense of well-being. They must go out in the sun more often; Morton was so city-pale, cooped up all week inside the gray factorylike university. She squeezed his arm affectionately and glanced at Larry, delighting in the

20 pointed little face frowning in concentration over the tunnel he was digging. The other boy suddenly stood up and with a quick, deliberate swing of his chubby arm threw a spadeful of sand at Larry. It just missed his head. Larry continued digging; the boy

25 remained standing, shovel raised, stolid and impassive.

"No, no, little boy." She shook her finger at him, her eyes searching for the child's mother or nurse. "We mustn't throw sand. It may get in someone's

30 eyes and hurt. We must play nicely in the nice sandbox." The boy looked at her in unblinking expectancy. He was about Larry's age but perhaps ten pounds heavier, a husky little boy with none of

Larry's quickness and sensitivity in his face. Where
35   was his mother? The only other people left in the
playground were two women and a little girl on
roller skates leaving now through the gate, and a
man on a bench a few feet away. He was a big man,
and he seemed to be taking up the whole bench as
40   he held the Sunday comics close to his face. She
supposed he was the child's father. He did not look
up from his comics, but spat once deftly out of the
corner of his mouth. She turned her eyes away.

At that moment, as swiftly as before, the fat little
45   boy threw another spadeful of sand at Larry. This
time some of it landed on his hair and forehead.
Larry looked up at his mother, his mouth tentative;
her expression would tell him whether to cry or not.

Her first instinct was to rush to her son, brush the
50   sand out of his hair, and punish the other child, but
she controlled it. She always said that she wanted
Larry to learn to fight his own battles.

"Don't *do* that, little boy," she said sharply,
leaning forward on the bench. "You mustn't throw
55   sand!"

The man on the bench moved his mouth as if to
spit again, but instead he spoke. He did not look at
her, but at the boy only.

"You go right ahead, Joe," he said loudly. "Throw
60   all you want. This here is a *public*
sandbox."

She felt a sudden weakness in her knees as she
glanced at Morton. He had become aware of what
was happening. He put his *Times* down carefully on
65   his lap and turned his fine, lean face toward the

man, smiling the shy, apologetic smile he might have offered a student in pointing out an error in his thinking. When he spoke to the man, it was with his usual reasonableness.

70   "You're quite right," he said pleasantly, "but just because this is a public place...."

The man lowered his funnies and looked at Morton. He looked at him from head to foot, slowly and deliberately. "Yeah?" His insolent voice

75   was edged with menace. "My kid's got just as good right here as yours, and if he feels like throwing sand, he'll throw it, and if you don't like it, you can take your kid the hell out of here."

The children were listening, their eyes and

80   mouths wide open, their spades forgotten in small fists. She noticed the muscle in Morton's jaw tighten. He was rarely angry; he seldom lost his temper. She was suffused with a tenderness for her husband and an impotent rage against the man for

85   involving him in a situation so alien and so distasteful to him.

"Now, just a minute," Morton said courteously, "you must realize...."

"Aw, shut up," said the man.

90   Her heart began to pound. Morton half rose; the *Times* slid to the ground. Slowly the other man stood up. He took a couple of steps toward Morton, then stopped. He flexed his great arms, waiting. She pressed her trembling knees together. Would there

95   be violence, fighting? How dreadful, how incredible.... She must do something, stop them, call for help. She wanted to put her hand on her

husband's sleeve, to pull him down, but for some reason she didn't.

100   Morton adjusted his glasses. He was very pale. "This is ridiculous," he said unevenly. "I must ask you...."

    "Oh, yeah?" said the man. He stood with his legs spread apart, rocking a little, looking at Morton
105 with utter scorn. "You and who else?"

    For a moment the two men looked at each other nakedly. Then Morton turned his back on the man and said quietly, "Come on, let's get out of here." He walked awkwardly, almost limping with self-
110 consciousness, to the sandbox. He stooped and lifted Larry and his shovel out.

    At once Larry came to life; his face lost its rapt expression and he began to kick and cry. "I don't want to go home, I want to play better, I don't *want*
115 any supper, I don't *like* supper...." It became a chant as they walked, pulling their child between them, his feet dragging on the ground. In order to get to the exit gate they had to pass the bench where the man sat sprawling again. She was careful not to look
120 at him. With all the dignity she could summon, she pulled Larry's sandy, perspiring little hand, while Morton pulled the other. Slowly and with head high she walked with her husband and child out of the playground.

125   Her first feeling was one of relief that a fight had been avoided, that no one was hurt. Yet beneath it there was a layer of something else, something heavy and inescapable. She sensed that it was more than just an unpleasant incident, more than defeat

130   of reason by force. She felt dimly it had something
      to do with her and Morton, something acutely
      personal, familiar, and important.

          Suddenly Morton spoke. "It wouldn't have proved
      anything."

135   "What?" she asked.

          "A fight. It wouldn't have proved anything
      beyond the fact that he's bigger than I am."

          "Of course," she said.

          "The only possible outcome," he continued
140   reasonably, "would have been—what? My glasses
      broken, perhaps a tooth or two replaced, a couple
      of days' work missed—and for what? For justice? For
      truth?"

          "Of course," she repeated. She quickened her
145   step. She wanted only to get home and to busy
      herself with her familiar tasks; perhaps then the
      feeling, glued like heavy plaster on her heart, would
      be gone. *Of all the stupid, despicable bullies*, she
      thought, pulling harder on Larry's hand. The child
150   was still crying. Always before she had felt a tender
      pity for his defenseless little body, the frail arms, the
      narrow shoulders with sharp, winglike shoulder
      blades, the thin and unsure legs, but now her mouth
      tightened in resentment.

155   "Stop crying," she said sharply. "I'm ashamed of
      you!" She felt as if all three of them were tracking
      mud along the street. The child cried louder.

          If there had been an issue involved, she thought, *if
      there had been something to fight for…. But what else
160   could he possibly have done? Allow himself to be beaten?
      Attempt to educate the man? Call a policeman? "Officer,*

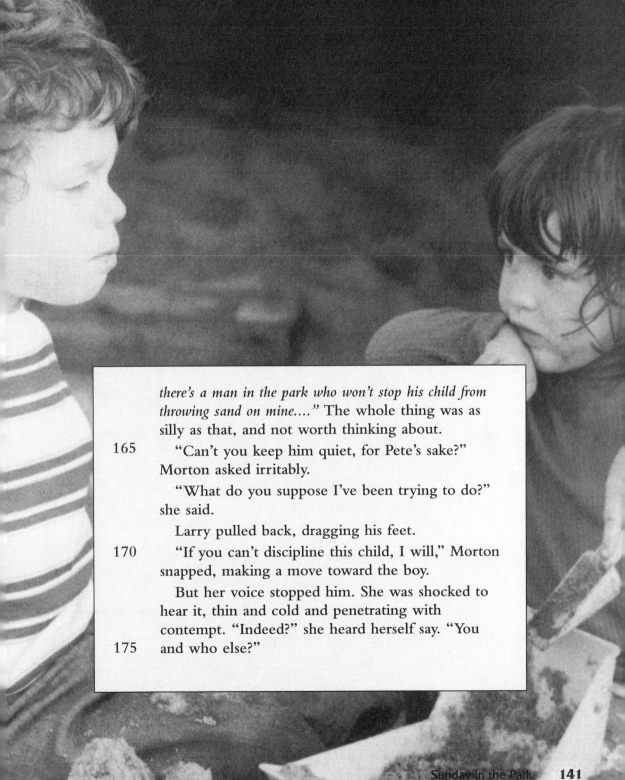

there's a man in the park who won't stop his child from throwing sand on mine...." The whole thing was as silly as that, and not worth thinking about.

165   "Can't you keep him quiet, for Pete's sake?" Morton asked irritably.

"What do you suppose I've been trying to do?" she said.

Larry pulled back, dragging his feet.

170   "If you can't discipline this child, I will," Morton snapped, making a move toward the boy.

But her voice stopped him. She was shocked to hear it, thin and cold and penetrating with contempt. "Indeed?" she heard herself say. "You

175   and who else?"

Sunday in the Park

Glossary

to muffle	to make less loud
to abandon	to leave
diligently	with care, and hard work
to be cooped up	to be kept inside
affectionately	with warmth and love
deliberate	on purpose
stolid	not showing emotion
impassive	not showing emotion
husky	strong, big
tentative	hesitant, not definite
funnies	comics
insolent	rude
menace	threatening to bring harm or danger
suffused	covered, filled with
impotent	powerless
courteous	polite
rapt	very intent and interested
despicable	deserving to be hated
frail	weak
resentment	to feel upset, angry, or insulted by something
to discipline	to train to be obedient, to punish

So What Are You, Anyway?

by Lawrence Hill

"Why do you keep asking me if my Dad is Negro? Yes, he's a Negro! Okay? OKAY? Negro Negro Negro!"

CAROLE SETTLES IN SEAT 12A, beside the window, puts her doll on a vacant seat and snaps open her purse. She holds up a mirror. She looks into her own dark eyes. She examines her handful of freckles, which are tiny ink spots dotting her cheeks. She checks for pimples, but finds none. Only the clear complexion that her father sometimes calls "milk milk milk milk chocolate" as he burrows into her neck with kisses.

"This is yours, I believe." A big man with a sunburnt face is holding her doll upside down.

"May I have her, please?" Carole says.

He turns the doll right side up. "A black doll! I never saw such a thing!"

"Her name's Amy. May I have her, please?"

"Henry Norton!" cries the man's wife. "Give that doll back this instant!"

Carole tucks the doll close to the window.

The man sits beside Carole. The woman takes the aisle seat.

"Don't mind him," the woman says, leaning towards Carole. "By the way, I'm Betty Norton, and he's my husband, Henry."

The man next to Carole hogs the armrest. His feet sprawl onto her side. And he keeps looking at her.

The stewardess passes by, checking seat belts. "Everything okay?"

"May I go to the bathroom?" Carole asks.

"Do you think you could wait? We're about to take off."

"Okay."

Carole looks out the window, sees the Toronto airport buildings fall behind and wonders if her parents are

watching. Say goodbye, she instructs Amy, waving the doll's hand, say goodbye to Mom and Dad. The engines charge to life. Her seat hums. They taxi down the runway. She feels a
35 hollowness in her stomach when they lift into the air. Her ears plug and stay that way until the plane levels out over pillows of cotton. They burn as bright as the sun. So that is what the other side of clouds look like!

"Excuse me. *Excuse me!*" The man is talking to her. "You
40 can go to the bathroom now, you know."

"No, that's all right," Carole says.

"Travelling all along, are you?"

Carole swallows with difficulty.

"Where do you live?" he asks.

45 "Don Mills."

"Oh, really?" he says. "Were you born there?"

"Yes."

"And your parents?"

"My mother was born in Chicago and my father was
50 born in Tucson."

"And you're going to visit your grandparents?"

She nods.

"And your parents let you travel alone!"

"It's only an airplane! And I'm a big girl."

55 The man lowers the back of his seat, chuckling. He whispers to his wife. "No!" Carole hears her whisper back, "*You* ask her!"

Carole yawns, holds Amy's hand and goes to sleep. The clinking of silverware wakens her, but she hears the man
60 and woman talking about her, so she keeps her eyes shut.

"I don't know, Henry," says the woman. "Don't ask me.

Ask *her*."

"I'm kind of curious," he says. "Aren't you?"

Carole can't make out the woman's answer. But then she hears her say:

"I just can't see it. It's not fair to children. I don't mind them mixed, but the world isn't ready for it. They're neither one thing nor the other. Henry, wake that child and see if she wants to eat."

When the man taps her shoulder, Carole opens her eyes. "I have to go to the bathroom," she says.

"But they're going to serve the meal," the man says.

"Henry! If she wants out, let her out. She's only a child."

Carole grimaces. She is definitely not a child. She is a young lady! She can identify Drambuie, Kahlua, and Grand Marnier by smell!

Once in the aisle, Carole realizes that she has forgotten Amy.

Henry Norton hands her the doll. "There you go. And don't fall out of the plane, now. There's a big hole down by the toilet."

"There is not!" Carole says. "There isn't any such thing!" She heads down the aisle with an eye out just in case there is a hole, after all.

Coming out of the toilet, Carole finds the stewardess. "Excuse me, miss. Could I sit somewhere else?"

The woman frowns. "Why?"

"I don't like the window."

"Is that it? Is that the only reason?"

"Well...yes."

"I'm sorry, but we don't have time to move you now. We're serving a meal. Ask me later, if you like."

After Carole had eaten and had her tray taken and been served a hot face towel, the man says: "What *are* you, anyway? My wife and I were wondering."

95

Carole blinks, sees the man's clear blue eyes and drops her head.

"What do you mean?" she says.

"You know, what are you? What race?"

100

Carole's mouth drops. Race? What is that? She doesn't understand. Yet she senses that the man is asking a bad question. It is as if he is asking her something dirty, or touching her in a bad place. She wishes her Mom and Dad were there. They could tell her what "race" meant.

105

"That doll of yours is black," Henry Norton says. "That's a Negro doll. That's race. Negro. What's your race?"

The question still confuses her.

"Put it this way," the man says. "What is your father?"

The question baffles her. What is her father? He is her

110

Dad! He is her Dad and every Sunday morning he makes pancakes for the whole family and lets Carole pour hot syrup on them and afterwards he sits her on his lap and tells stories.

Mrs. Norton leans towards Carole. "Say you had a

115

colouring book. What colour would you make your Dad?"

"I never use just one colour."

"Okay. What colour would you make his face?"

"Brown."

"And your mother?"

120

Carole imagines a blank page. What would she put in her mother's face? She has to put something in there. She can't just leave it blank. "I don't know."

"Sure you do," Mrs. Norton says. "How would you

colour your mother's face?"

125 "Yellow."

Carole sees Mr. and Mrs. Norton look at each other.

"Is your mother Chinese?" Mrs. Norton asks.

"No."

"Are you sure you'd colour her yellow?"

130 "No."

"What else might you colour her?"

What else? Carole feels ashamed at her stupidity. A tear races down her cheek. "Red," she says, finally.

"Red! You can't colour a face red! Is your mother white?

135 Is she like me? Her face! Is it the same colour as mine?"

"Yes."

"And your father's brown?"

Carole nods.

"When you say brown, do you mean he is a Negro?"

140 "Yes." Of course her father is a Negro. If Mrs. Norton wanted to know all along if her Dad was a Negro, why didn't she just ask?

"So you're mixed?" Mrs. Norton says. "You're a mulatto!"

145 Carole's lip quivers. What is mulatto? Why do they keep asking her what she is? She isn't anything!

"So is that it? You're a mulatto? You know what a mulatto is, don't you? Haven't your parents taught you that word?"

150 Approaching with a cart of juice, the stewardess looks up and smiles at Carole. That gives her a rush of courage.

"Leave me alone!" she screams at Mrs. Norton.

Passengers stare. The stewardess spills a drink. Mrs.

Norton sits back hard in her seat, her hands raised, fingers
155   spread. Carole sees people watching.

"Why do you keep asking me if my Dad is Negro? Yes,
he's a Negro! Okay? OKAY? Negro Negro Negro!"

"Calm down," Mrs. Norton says, reaching over.

"Don't touch her," the stewardess says.

160   "Who are these people?" someone says from across the
aisle. "Imagine, talking to a child like that, and in 1970!"

One woman sitting in front of Carole stands up and turns
around.

"Would you like to come and sit with me, little girl?"

165   "No!" Carole shouts. "I don't like all these questions.
She keeps asking me how I would colour my parents in a
colouring book! Why do you keep asking me that?"

Mrs. Norton pleads with Carole to stop.

"How would you like it if that happened to you?" Carole
170   says. "So what are you, anyway? What are your parents?
How would you colour them? Well, I don't care! I don't
even care!"

"How would you like to come and sit with me?" the
stewardess says, smiling. "I'll make you a special drink.
175   Have you ever had a Shirley Temple?"

Carole nods enthusiastically. Already she feels better.
Clutching Amy, she passes by the Nortons, who swing their
legs to let her out.

"My God," Carole hears Mrs. Norton tell her husband,
180   "talk about sensitive."

So What Are You, Anyway?

Glossary

to hog	to greedily take more than one needs
to chuckle	to laugh quietly
to clink	to make a thin sharp sound like glass striking against glass
to grimace	to make a face in displeasure or pain
Drambuie, Kahlua, Grand Marnier	names of liqueurs
mulatto	someone who has one white parent and one black parent

Dry September

by William Faulkner

"Believe, hell!" a hulking youth in a sweat-stained silk shirt said. *"Won't you take a white woman's word before a nigger's?"*

Background:

Dry September is poetically written, with difficult vocabulary, but the exciting, fast-moving plot makes this story a pleasure to read. The use of force is demonstrated on different levels. Patterns of power and powerlessness, of conflict between individuals and groups, women and men, black and white build up to a climax of physical violence.

Warm-up Discussion/Response Journal:

1. Write down any words that you associate with the title, *Dry September.* Make a list with your partner or group. Let your imagination and memory work freely as you list adjectives, nouns, and verbs which relate somehow to the words "dry" and "September."

2. Then read, or listen to your teacher read, the first paragraph of this story. List the words that you find most striking and important. Compare them with your group's lists. What do you think this story will be about?

3. Because this story is a long one, you will read it section by section. William Faulkner himself divided the story up into five sections. Read each section once quickly without using a dictionary. It is not necessary that you understand every word. Just concentrate on understanding the main ideas of the story. Then re-read that section more carefully in order to answer the questions.

THROUGH THE BLOODY SEPTEMBER TWILIGHT, aftermath of sixty-two rainless days, it had gone like a fire in dry grass-the rumor, the story, whatever it was. Something about Miss Minnie Cooper and a Negro. Attacked, insulted, frightened: none of them, gathered in the barber shop on that Saturday evening where the ceiling fan stirred, without freshening it, the vitiated air, sending back upon them, in recurrent surges of stale pomade and lotion, their own stale breath and odors, knew exactly what had happened.

"Except it wasn't Will Mayes," a barber said. He was a man of middle age; a thin, sand-colored man with a mild face, who was shaving a client. "I know Will Mayes. He's a good nigger. And I know Miss Minnie Cooper, too."

"What do you know about her?" a second barber said.

"Who is she?" the client said. "A young girl?"

"No," the barber said. "She's about forty, I reckon. She ain't married. That's why I dont believe—"

"Believe, hell!" a hulking youth in a sweat-stained silk shirt said. "Wont you take a white woman's word before a nigger's?"

"I dont believe Will Mayes did it," the barber said. "I know Will Mayes."

"Maybe you know who did it, then. Maybe you already got him out of town, you damn niggerlover."

"I dont believe anybody did anything. I dont believe anything happened. I leave it to you fellows if them ladies that get old without getting married dont have notions that man cant—"

"Then you are a hell of a white man," the client said. He moved under the cloth. The youth had sprung to his feet.

"You dont?" he said. "Do you accuse a white woman of lying?"

The barber held the razor poised above the half-risen

client. He did not look around.

35   "It's this durn weather," another said. "It's enough to make a man do anything. Even to her."

Nobody laughed. The barber said in his mild, stubborn tone: "I aint accusing nobody of nothing. I just know and you fellows know how a woman that never–"

40   "You damn niggerlover!" the youth said.

"Shut up, Butch," another said. "We'll get the facts in plenty of time to act."

"Who is? Who's getting them?" the youth said. "Facts, hell I–"

45   "You're a fine white man," the client said. "Aint you?" In his frothy beard he looked like a desert rat in the moving pictures. "You tell them, Jack," he said to the youth. "If there aint any white men in this town, you can count on me, even if I aint only a drummer and a stranger."

50   "That's right, boys," the barber said. "Find out the truth first. I know Will Mayes."

"Well, by God!" the youth shouted. "To think that a white man in this town–"

"Shut up, Butch," the second speaker said. "We got plenty
55   of time."

The client sat up. He looked at the speaker. "Do you claim that anything excuses a nigger attacking a white woman? Do you mean to tell me you are a white man and you'll stand for it? You better go back North where you came from. The
60   South dont want your kind here."

"North what?" the second said. "I was born and raised in this town."

"Well, by God!" the youth said. He looked about with a strained, baffled gaze, as if he was trying to remember what it
65   was he wanted to say or to do. He drew his sleeve across his sweating face. "Damn if I'm going to let a white woman–"

"You tell them, Jack," the drummer said. "By God, if
they—"

The screen door crashed open. A man stood in the floor,
his feet apart and his heavy-set body poised easily. His white
shirt was open at the throat; he wore a felt hat. His hot, bold
glance swept the group. His name was McLendon. He had
commanded troops at the front in France and had been
decorated for valor.

"Well," he said, "are you going to sit there and let a black
son rape a white woman on the streets of Jefferson?"

Butch sprang up again. The silk of his shirt clung flat to his
heavy shoulders. At each armpit was a dark halfmoon.
"That's what I been telling them! That's what I—"

"Did it really happen?" a third said. "This aint the first
man scare she ever had, like Hawkshaw says. Wasn't there
something about a man on the kitchen roof, watching her
undress, about a year ago?"

"What?" the client said. "What's that?" The barber had
been slowly forcing him back into the chair; he arrested
himself reclining, his head lifted, the barber still pressing him
down.

McLendon whirled on the third speaker. "Happen? What
the hell difference does it make? Are you going to let the
black sons get away with it until one really does it?"

"That's what I'm telling them!" Butch shouted. He cursed,
long and steady, pointless.

"Here, here," a fourth said. "Not so loud. Dont talk so
loud."

"Sure," McLendon said; "no talking necessary at all. I've
done my talking. Who's with me?" He poised on the balls of
his feet, roving his gaze.

The barber held the drummer's face down, the razor
poised. "Find out the facts first, boys. I know Willy Mayes. It

100 wasn't him. Let's get the sheriff and do this thing right."

McLendon whirled upon him his furious, rigid face. The barber did not look away. They looked like men of different races. The other barbers had ceased also above their prone clients. "You mean to tell me," McLendon said, "that you'd
105 take a nigger's word before a white woman's? Why, you damn niggerloving–"

The third speaker rose and grasped McLendon's arm; he too had been a soldier. "Now, now. Let's figure this thing out. Who knows anything about what really happened?"
110 "Figure out hell!" McLendon jerked his arm free. "All that're with me get up from there. The ones that aint–" He roved his gaze, dragging his sleeve across his face.

Three men rose. The drummer in the chair sat up. "Here," he said, jerking at the cloth about his neck; "get this rag off
115 me. I'm with him. I don't live here, but by God, if our mothers and wives and sisters–" He smeared the cloth over his face and flung it to the floor. McLendon stood in the floor and cursed the others. Another rose and moved toward him. The remainder sat uncomfortable, not looking at one
120 another, then one by one they rose and joined him.

The barber picked the cloth from the floor. He began to fold it neatly. "Boys, don't do that. Will Mayes never done it. I know."

"Come on," McLendon said. He whirled. From his hip
125 pocket protruded the butt of a heavy automatic pistol. They went out. The screen door crashed behind them reverberant in the dead air.

The barber wiped the razor carefully and swiftly, and put it away, and ran to the rear, and took his hat from the wall. "I'll
130 be back as soon as I can," he said to the other barbers. "I cant let–" He went out, running. The two other barbers followed him to the door and caught it on the rebound,

leaning out and looking up the street after him. The air was flat and dead. It had a metallic taste at the base of the tongue.

135   "What can he do?" the first said. The second one was saying "Jees Christ" under his breath. "I'd just as lief be Will Mayes as Hawk, if he gets McLendon riled."

"Jees Christ, Jees Christ," the second whispered.

"You reckon he really done it to her?" the first said.

140   II

She was thirty-eight or thirty-nine. She lived in a small frame house with her invalid mother and a thin, sallow, unflagging aunt, where each morning between ten and eleven she would appear on the porch in a lace-trimmed boudoir
145   cap, to sit swinging in the porch swing until noon. After dinner she lay down for a while, until the afternoon began to cool. Then, in one of the three or four new voile dresses which she had each summer, she would go downtown to spend the afternoon in the stores with the other ladies, where
150   they would handle the goods and haggle over the prices in cold immediate voices, without any intention of buying.

She was of comfortable people—not the best in Jefferson, but good people enough—and she was still on the slender side of ordinary looking, with a bright, faintly haggard manner
155   and dress. When she was young she had a slender, nervous body and a sort of hard vivacity which enabled her for a time to ride upon the crest of the town's social life as exemplified by the high school party and church social period of her contemporaries while still children enough to be
160   unclassconscious.

She was the last to realize that she was losing ground; that those among whom she had been a little brighter and louder flame than any other were beginning to learn the pleasure of snobbery—male—and retaliation—female. That was when her
165   face began to wear that bright, haggard look. She still carried

it to parties on shadowy porticoes and summer lawns, like a
mask or a flag, with the bafflement of furious repudiation of
truth in her eyes. One evening at a party she heard a boy and
two girls, all schoolmates, talking. She never accepted
170 another invitation.

She watched the girls with whom she had grown up as
they married and got homes and children, but no man ever
called on her steadily until the children of the other girls had
been calling her "aunty" for several years, the while their
175 mothers told them in bright voices about how popular Aunt
Minnie had been as a girl. Then the town began to see her
driving on Sunday afternoons with the cashier in the bank.
He was a widower of about forty—a high-colored man,
smelling always faintly of the barber shop or of whisky. He
180 owned the first automobile in town, a red runabout; Minnie
had the first motoring bonnet and veil the town ever saw.
Then the town began to say: "Poor Minnie." "But she is old
enough to take care of herself," others said. That was when
she began to ask her old schoolmates that their children call
185 her "cousin" instead of "aunty."

It was twelve years now since she had been relegated into
adultery by public opinion, and eight years since the cashier
had gone to a Memphis bank, returning for one day each
Christmas, which he spent at an annual bachelors' party at a
190 hunting club on the river. From behind their curtains the
neighbors would see the party pass, and during the over-the-
way Christmas day visiting they would tell her about him,
about how well he looked, and how they heard that he was
prospering in the city, watching with bright, secret eyes her
195 haggard, bright face. Usually by that hour there would be a
scent of whisky on her breath. It was supplied her by a
youth, a clerk at the soda fountain: "Sure; I buy it for the old
gal. I reckon she's entitled to a little fun."

Her mother kept to her room altogether now; the gaunt

200 aunt ran the house. Against that background Minnie's bright dresses, her idle and empty days, had a quality of furious unreality. She went out in the evenings only with women now, neighbors, to the moving pictures. Each afternoon she dressed in one of the new dresses and went downtown alone,
205 where her young "cousins" were already strolling in the late afternoons with their delicate, silken heads and thin, awkward arms and conscious hips, clinging to one another or shrieking and giggling with paired boys in the soda fountain when she passed and went on along the serried store fronts, in the
210 doors of which the sitting and lounging men did not even follow her with their eyes any more.

III

The barber went swiftly up the street where the sparse lights, insect-swirled, glared in rigid and violent suspension in
215 the lifeless air. The day had died in a pall of dust; above the darkened square, shrouded by the spent dust, the sky was as clear as the inside of a brass bell. Below the east was a rumour of the twice-waxed moon.

When he overtook them McLendon and three others were
220 getting into a car parked in an alley. McLendon stooped his thick head, peering out beneath the top. "Changed your mind, did you?" he said. "Damn good thing; by God, tomorrow when this town hears about how you talked tonight-"
225 "Now, now," the other ex-soldier said. "Hawkshaw's all right. Come on, Hawk; jump in."

"Will Mayes never done it, boys," the barber said. "If anybody done it. Why, you all know well as I do there aint any town where they got better niggers than us. And you
230 know how a lady will kind of think things about men when there aint any reason to, and Miss Minnie anyway-"

"Sure, sure," the soldier said. "We're just going to talk to him a little; that's all."

"Talk hell!" Butch said. "When we're through with the–"

235   "Shut up, for God's sake!" the soldier said. "Do you want everybody in town–"

"Tell them, by God!" McLendon said. "Tell every one of the sons that'll let a white woman–"

"Let's go; let's go: here's the other car." The second car slid

240   squealing out of a cloud of dust at the alley mouth. McLendon started his car and took the lead. Dust lay like fog in the street. The street lights hung nimbused as in water. They drove on out of town.

A rutted lane turned at right angles. Dust hung above it

245   too, and above all the land. The dark bulk of the ice plant, where the Negro Mayes was night watchman, rose against the sky. "Better stop here, hadn't we?" the soldier said, McLendon did not reply. He hurled the car up and slammed to a stop, the headlights glaring on the blank wall.

250   "Listen here, boys," the barber said; "if he's here, don't that prove he never done it? Dont it? If it was him, he would run. Dont you see he would?" The second car came up and stopped. McLendon got down; Butch sprang down beside him. "Listen, boys," the barber said.

255   "Cut the lights off!" McLendon said. The breathless dark rushed down. There was no sound in it save their lungs as they sought air in the parched dust in which for two months they had lived; then the diminishing crunch of McLendon's and Butch's feet, and a moment later McLendon's voice:

260   "Will ... Will!"

Below the east the wan hemorrhage of the moon increased. It heaved above the ridge, silvering the air, the dust, so that they seemed to breathe, live, in a bowl of molted lead. There was no sound of nightbird nor insect, no

265   sound save their breathing and a faint ticking of contracting metal about the cars. When their bodies touched one another

they seemed to sweat dryly, for no more moisture came. "Christ!" a voice said; "let's get out of here."

But they didn't move until vague noises began to grow out
270 of the darkness ahead; then they got out and waited tensely
in the breathless dark. There was another sound: a blow, a
hissing expulsion of breath and McLendon cursing in
undertone. They stood a moment longer, then they ran
forward. They ran in a stumbling clump, as though they were
275 fleeing something. "Kill him, kill the son," a voice whispered.
McLendon flung them back.

"Not here," he said. "Get him into the car." "Kill him, kill
the black son!" the voice murmured. They dragged the
Negro to the car. The barber had waited beside the car. He
280 could feel himself sweating and he knew he was going to be
sick at the stomach.

"What is it, captains?" the Negro said. "I aint done
nothing. 'Fore God, Mr John." Someone produced handcuffs.
They worked busily about the Negro as though he were a
285 post, quiet, intent, getting in one another's way. He submitted
to the handcuffs, looking swiftly and constantly from dim
face to dim face. "Who's here, captains?" he said, leaning to
peer into the faces until they could feel his breath and smell
his sweaty reek. He spoke a name or two. "What you all say
290 I done, Mr John?"

McLendon jerked the car door open. "Get in!" he said.

The Negro did not move. "What you all going to do with
me, Mr John? I aint done nothing. White folks, captains, I
aint done nothing: I swear 'fore God." He called another
295 name.

"Get in!" McLendon said. He struck the Negro. The
others expelled their breath in a dry hissing and struck him
with random blows and he whirled and cursed them, and
swept back his manacled hands across their faces and slashed
300 the barber upon the mouth, and the barber struck him also.

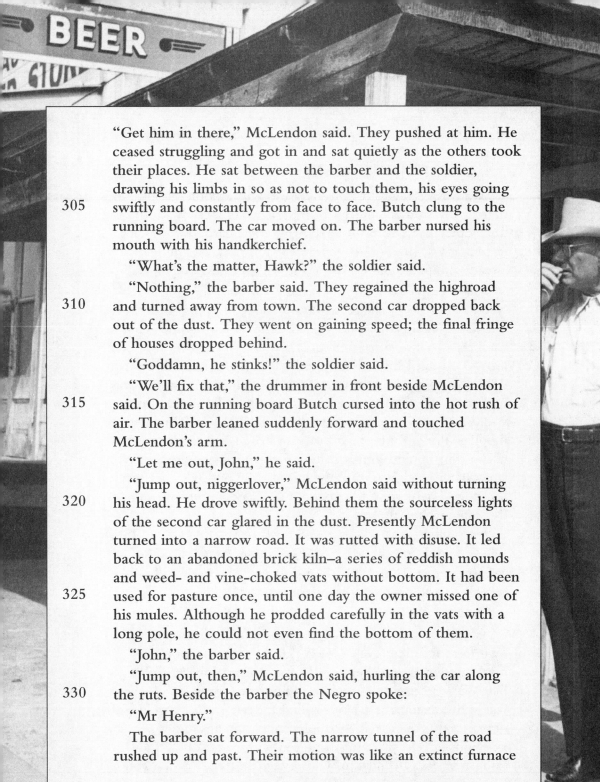

"Get him in there," McLendon said. They pushed at him. He ceased struggling and got in and sat quietly as the others took their places. He sat between the barber and the soldier, drawing his limbs in so as not to touch them, his eyes going
305 swiftly and constantly from face to face. Butch clung to the running board. The car moved on. The barber nursed his mouth with his handkerchief.

"What's the matter, Hawk?" the soldier said.

"Nothing," the barber said. They regained the highroad
310 and turned away from town. The second car dropped back out of the dust. They went on gaining speed; the final fringe of houses dropped behind.

"Goddamn, he stinks!" the soldier said.

"We'll fix that," the drummer in front beside McLendon
315 said. On the running board Butch cursed into the hot rush of air. The barber leaned suddenly forward and touched McLendon's arm.

"Let me out, John," he said.

"Jump out, niggerlover," McLendon said without turning
320 his head. He drove swiftly. Behind them the sourceless lights of the second car glared in the dust. Presently McLendon turned into a narrow road. It was rutted with disuse. It led back to an abandoned brick kiln–a series of reddish mounds and weed- and vine-choked vats without bottom. It had been
325 used for pasture once, until one day the owner missed one of his mules. Although he prodded carefully in the vats with a long pole, he could not even find the bottom of them.

"John," the barber said.

"Jump out, then," McLendon said, hurling the car along
330 the ruts. Beside the barber the Negro spoke:

"Mr Henry."

The barber sat forward. The narrow tunnel of the road rushed up and past. Their motion was like an extinct furnace

335 blast: cooler, but utterly dead. The car bounded from rut to rut.

"Mr Henry," the Negro said.

The barber began to tug furiously at the door. "Look out, there!" the soldier said, but the barber had already kicked the door open and swung onto the running board. The soldier
340 leaned across the Negro and grasped at him, but he had already jumped. The car went on without checking speed.

The impetus hurled him crashing through dust-sheathed weeds, into the ditch. Dust puffed about him, and in a thin vicious crackling of sapless stems he lay choking and retching
345 until the second car passed and died away. Then he rose and limped on until he reached the highroad and turned toward town, brushing at his clothes with his hands. The moon was higher, riding high and clear of the dust at last, and after a while the town began to glare beneath the dust. He went on,
350 limping. Presently he heard cars and the glow of them grew in the dust behind him and he left the road and crouched again in the weeds until they passed. McLendon's car came last now. There were four people in it and Butch was not on the running board.

355 They went on; the dust swallowed them; the glare and the sound died away. The dust of them hung for a while, but soon the eternal dust absorbed it again. The barber climbed back onto the road and limped on toward town.

IV

360 As she dressed for supper on that Saturday evening, her own flesh felt like fever. Her hands trembled among the hooks and eyes, and her eyes had a feverish look, and her hair swirled crisp and crackling under the comb. While she was still dressing the friends called for her and sat while she
365 donned her sheerest underthings and stockings and a new voile dress. "Do you feel strong enough to go out?" they said, their eyes bright too, with a dark glitter. "When you

have had time to get over the shock, you must tell us what happened. What he said and did; everything."

370   In the leafed darkness, as they walked toward the square, she began to breathe deeply, something like a swimmer preparing to dive, until she ceased trembling, the four of them walking slowly because of the terrible heat and out of
375   solicitude for her. But as they neared the square she began to tremble again, walking with her head up, her hands clenched at her sides, their voices about her murmurous, also with that feverish, glittering quality of their eyes.

They entered the square, she in the center of the group, fragile in her fresh dress. She was trembling worse. She
380   walked slower and slower, as children eat ice cream, her head up and her eyes bright in the haggard banner of her face, passing the hotel and the coatless drummers in chairs along the curb looking around at her: "That's the one: see? The one in pink in the middle." "Is that her? What did they do
385   with the nigger? Did they–?" "Sure. He's all right." "All right, is he?" "Sure. He went on a little trip." Then the drug store, where even the young men lounging in the doorway tipped their hats and followed with their eyes the motion of her hips and legs when she passed.

390   They went on, passing the lifted hats of the gentlemen, the suddenly ceased voices, deferent, protective. "Do you see?" the friends said. Their voices sounded like long, hovering sighs of hissing exultation. "There's not a Negro on the square. Not one."

395   They reached the picture show. It was like a miniature fairyland with its lighted lobby and colored lithographs of life caught in its terrible and beautiful mutations. Her lips began to tingle. In the dark, when the picture began, it would be all
400   right; she could hold back the laughing so it would not waste away so fast and so soon. So she hurried on before the turning faces, the undertones of low astonishment, and they

took their accustomed places where she could see the aisle against the silver glare and the young men and girls coming in two and two against it.

The lights flicked away; the screen glowed silver, and soon life began to unfold, beautiful and passionate and sad, while still the young men and girls entered, scented and sibilant in the half dark, their paired backs in silhouette delicate and sleek, their slim, quick bodies awkward, divinely young, while beyond them the silver dream accumulated, inevitably on and on. She began to laugh. In trying to suppress it, it made more noise than ever; heads began to turn. Still laughing, her friends raised her and led her out, and she stood at the curb, laughing on a high, sustained note, until the taxi came up and they helped her in.

They removed the pink voile and the sheer underthings and the stockings, and put her to bed, and cracked ice for her temples, and sent for the doctor. He was hard to locate, so they ministered to her with hushed ejaculations, renewing the ice and fanning her. While the ice was fresh and cold she stopped laughing and lay still for a time, moaning only a little. But soon the laughing welled again and her voice rose screaming.

"Shhhhhhhhhh! Shhhhhhhhhhhhhh!" they said, freshening the icepack, smoothing her hair, examining it for gray; "poor girl!" Then to one another: "Do you suppose anything really happened?" their eyes darkly aglitter, secret and passionate. "Shhhhhhhhhh! Poor girl! Poor Minnie!"

V

It was midnight when McLendon drove up to his neat new house. It was trim and fresh as a birdcage and almost as small, with its clean, green-and-white paint. He locked the car and mounted the porch and entered. His wife rose from a chair beside the reading lamp. McLendon stopped in the floor and stared at her until she looked down.

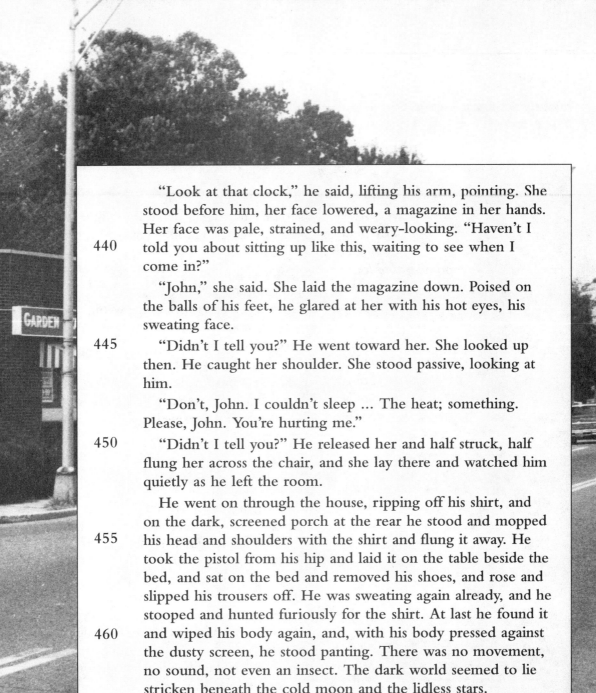

"Look at that clock," he said, lifting his arm, pointing. She stood before him, her face lowered, a magazine in her hands. Her face was pale, strained, and weary-looking. "Haven't I told you about sitting up like this, waiting to see when I come in?"

"John," she said. She laid the magazine down. Poised on the balls of his feet, he glared at her with his hot eyes, his sweating face.

"Didn't I tell you?" He went toward her. She looked up then. He caught her shoulder. She stood passive, looking at him.

"Don't, John. I couldn't sleep ... The heat; something. Please, John. You're hurting me."

"Didn't I tell you?" He released her and half struck, half flung her across the chair, and she lay there and watched him quietly as he left the room.

He went on through the house, ripping off his shirt, and on the dark, screened porch at the rear he stood and mopped his head and shoulders with the shirt and flung it away. He took the pistol from his hip and laid it on the table beside the bed, and sat on the bed and removed his shoes, and rose and slipped his trousers off. He was sweating again already, and he stooped and hunted furiously for the shirt. At last he found it and wiped his body again, and, with his body pressed against the dusty screen, he stood panting. There was no movement, no sound, not even an insect. The dark world seemed to lie stricken beneath the cold moon and the lidless stars.

440
445
450
455
460

Dry September

Glossary

Part I

twilight	the time when day is about to become night
aftermath	the result or period following an event
vitiated	spoiled, bad
pomade and lotion	perfumed hair and skin products
hulking	big, heavy and awkward
accuse	to charge someone with doing wrong or breaking the law
stand for it	to accept something
baffled	so confused that you can't act
poised	ready to act or move
remainder	what is left over; the rest
reverberant	causing a sound to repeat again and again; echoing

Part II

invalid	a person made weak by illness
slender	delicately or gracefully thin
haggard	having lines on the face and hollow places around the eyes as if through tiredness; looking very tired
vivacity	being full of life and high spirits
snobbery	the behaviour of a snob (someone who dislikes those he or she feels to be of lower social class, and admires people of a higher social class)
retaliate	to pay back evil with evil or wrong with wrong; to revenge
relegate	to put into a lower or worse position
adultery	sexual relations between a married person and someone outside the marriage
prosper	to become successful
idle	lazy; not working
lounge	to pass time doing nothing; to stand or sit in a lazy manner

Part III

squeal	to make a long, very high sound or cry
rut	a deep narrow track left in soft ground by a wheel
diminish	to become or seem smaller
tick	to make a regularly repeated short sound (like a clock or watch)
contract	to become smaller
blow	a hard stroke with the hand or a weapon
murmur	to make a soft sound or speak in a quiet voice
handcuffs	metal rings joined together, for fastening the wrists of a criminal
random	made or done aimlessly, without any plan
running board	a kind of step on the side of older cars, used when getting into the car
kiln	a box-shaped oven used for baking bricks
vat	a tank or very large container for holding liquids

Part IV

tremble	to shake uncontrollably (often from fear)
don	to put on (clothing)
solicitude	care, concern
fragile	easily broken or damaged
deferent	courteous, polite
miniature	very small (especially of something copied)
mutation	change
sibilant	producing or having a hissing sound (especially /s/ and /z/ sounds)
silhouette	shadow-like shape of something
inevitable	cannot be prevented from happening
suppress	to prevent from appearing or being expressed
ejaculation	something said suddenly
aglitter	glittering, shining brightly

Part V

trim	tidy, neat in appearance
pant	to take quick short breaths, especially after great effort or during great heat
stricken	affected or overcome by something, such as emotion, shock, or grief

Comprehension Check

1. Re-read the first paragraph. What do the following words refer to:

    "it" (line 2)

    "attacked, insulted, frightened" (line 4)

    "it" (line 6)

    What are the subject, verb, and object of the last sentence of the first paragraph?

2. True or False?

    _____ a.   The men's conversation takes place in a restaurant.

    _____ b.   It is early morning.

    _____ c.   The men are arguing about whether or not Will Mayes, a black man, attacked Miss Minnie Cooper.

    _____ d.   Miss Minnie Cooper is black.

    _____ e.   The weather has been unseasonably cold recently.

    _____ f.   McClendon is a big, powerful man.

    _____ g.   In the end, all the customers leave with McClendon to find Will Mayes.

3. Complete the following chart about the customers:

    Group A, led by McClendon   Group B, led by _____

    Names: 1. _____   1. _____

    　　　　2. _____

    　　　　3. _____

    What the group wants to do:

    The group's reasons:

    Their attitude:

4. The character of McClendon:

   a. Your adjectives to describe him   Details in the text that support your description

   _____   _____

   _____   _____

   _____   _____

   b. What effect does he have on the other men?

   c. Explain the following statement:

   "They looked like men of different races" (line 105)

Response Check

What is your emotional response to the character of McClendon? Hawkshaw? How does this first section make you feel?

PART II

Comprehension and Interpretation

Part II describes Miss Minnie Cooper's personal background. Describe her according to the following headings:

Miss Minnie Cooper

1. Appearance

2. Daily lifestyle

3. History

   a. Paragraphs 2 and 3–what change occurs in her life?

   b. "a boy and two girls . . . talking." What do you think she heard them say?

   c. Describe her relationship with the Memphis banker.

   d. What is the townspeople's attitude toward Minnie?

   e. Why don't the men watch her anymore?

Response Check

Do you like Minnie Cooper? Do you know anyone like her?

Comprehension and Interpretation

1. Look at the first paragraph and circle all the words that have a connotation of dying and death.

2. Draw a picture of the seating arrangement in McClendon's car. There are six men in the car. The first paragraph on page 163 will help you to do this.

3. Page 164, 4th paragraph:

   The barber began to tug furiously at the door. "Look out, there!" the soldier said, but the barber had already kicked the door open and swung onto the running boahe soldier leaned across the Negro and grasped at him, but he had already jumped. The car went on without checking speed.

   Who is "him"? "he"?

4. Plot: Put the following sentences in the correct order. Number one is done for you.

   a. Hawkshaw feels sick to his stomach.

   b. Will gets into the car.

   c. Hawkshaw jumps out of the car.

   d. Hawkshaw finds McClendon and three others and gets into the car.   1

   e. While Hawkshaw is hiding at the roadside, McClendon's car passes him.

   f. The men drive to an abandoned kiln.

   g. When McLendon and the others strike Will, Will strikes back.

   h. Will insists that he hasn't done anything wrong.

   i. Hawkshaw strikes Will.

   j. The men kill Will.

   k. Hawkshaw walks back to town.

   l. Hawkshaw tries to persuade the men not to hunt or harm Will.

   m. McClendon and Butch drag Will to the car.

5. How did Will die? How do you know?

Response Check

How would you describe the mood of Part III? Do you blame Will for hitting back? Do you blame Hawkshaw for hitting Will?

Comprehension and Interpretation

A. Choose the best possible answer:

1. Minnie's clothing for supper and the theatre is

    a. simple
    b. sexy
    c. bright

2. Minnie and her women friends are "feverish" from

    a. the heat
    b. sickness
    c. excitement

3. As she passes, the men

    a. ignore her
    b. say hello
    c. watch her body

4. The movie theatre is filled with

    a. housewives
    b. young couples
    c. families

5. The movie is probably

    a. a romance
    b. an adventure film
    c. a cowboy film

6. As she watches the movie, Minnie

    a. starts to cry
    b. starts to laugh
    c. faints

7. As her friends put ice on her head, they

    a. talk to the doctor
    b. check to see if she has any gray hair
    c. sympathize with her

B. 1. How and why has the men's attitude to Minnie changed?
    2. Describe Minnie's friends' attitude to her.
    3. Why does Minnie start to laugh hysterically?

Comprehension and Interpretation

1. Compare and contrast:

   McClendon's character and his house

   McClendon's character and his wife's character

   McClendon's treatment of Will and his treatment of his wife

2. ". . . with his body pressed against the dusty screen, he stood panting. There was no movement, no sound, not even an insect. The dark world seemed to lie stricken beneath the cold moon and the lidless stars."

   How do you think McClendon feels? What is he thinking about? How do the surroundings reflect his condition, and the condition of other characters in the story?

Interpretation: A Closer Look at Language

Sit in small groups. Each group should re-read one story section, looking for adjectives or phrases which evoke the five senses. When you are ready, write your group's findings on the board. A few examples are done for you.

	I	II	III	IV	V
feeling/touching				*heat*	
tasting	*metallic taste*				
smelling		*whiskey*			
seeing			*sparse lights*		
hearing					*no sound*

Close your eyes as the teacher or a student reads aloud each group's words for each section, and try to visualize and feel the setting. Then take 10 minutes and write a journal response. You may wish to write a summary of the sensual images of one section, or to express your own response to one or more of the sections of the story, or to describe an experience from your own life which you are reminded of.

Evaluation: Discussion or Response Journal

1. Choose one or more of the following poetic images from the story, or find another one which impressed you in the story. Explain the simile or metaphor and how it is effective.

    bloody September twilight
    like a fire in dry grass–the rumor
    the day had died in a pall of dust
    the wan hemorrhage of the moon increased
    the haggard banner of her face

2. List the "victims" of this story. How are they similar? How are they different?

First Practice

by Gary Gildner

First Practice

After the doctor checked to see
we weren't ruptured,
the man with the short cigar took us
under the grade school,
5   where we went in case of attack
or storm, and said
he was Clifford Hill, he was
a man who believed dogs
ate dogs, he had once killed
10   for his country, and if
there were any girls present
for them to leave now.   No one
left. OK, he said, he said I take
15   that to mean you are hungry
men who hate to lose as much
as I do. OK. Then
he made two lines of us
facing each other,
20   and across the way, he said,
is the man you hate most
in the world,
and if we are to win
that title I want to see how.
25   But I don't want to see
any marks when you're dressed,
he said. He said, *Now.*

Gary Gildner

What Do I Remember of the Evacuation?

by Joy Kogawa

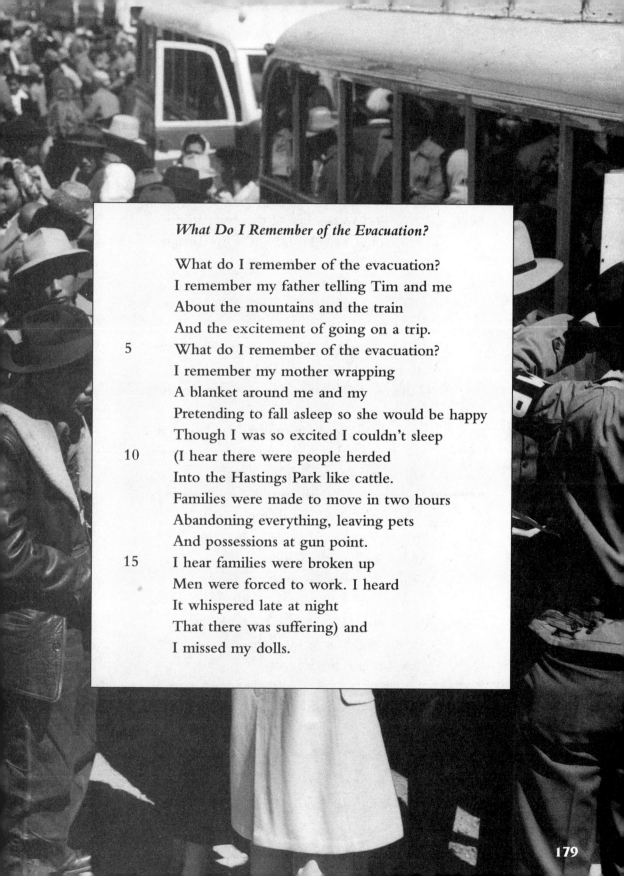

What Do I Remember of the Evacuation?

What do I remember of the evacuation?
I remember my father telling Tim and me
About the mountains and the train
And the excitement of going on a trip.
5   What do I remember of the evacuation?
I remember my mother wrapping
A blanket around me and my
Pretending to fall asleep so she would be happy
Though I was so excited I couldn't sleep
10   (I hear there were people herded
Into the Hastings Park like cattle.
Families were made to move in two hours
Abandoning everything, leaving pets
And possessions at gun point.
15   I hear families were broken up
Men were forced to work. I heard
It whispered late at night
That there was suffering) and
I missed my dolls.

20   What do I remember of the evacuation?
         I remember Miss Foster and Miss Tucker
         Who still live in Vancouver
         And who did what they could
         And loved the children and who gave me
25   A puzzle to play with on the train.
         And I remember the mountains and I was
         Six years old and I swear I saw a giant
         Gulliver of Gulliver's Travels scanning the
          horizon
30   And when I told my mother she believed it too
         And I remember how careful my parents were
         Not to bruise us with bitterness
         And I remember the puzzle of Lorraine Life
         Who said "Don't insult me" when I
35   Proudly wrote my name in Japanese
         And Tim flew the Union Jack
         When the war was over but Lorraine
         And her friends spat on us anyway
         And I prayed to the God who loves
40   All the children in his sight
         That I might be white.

Joy Kogawa

Much Madness is Divinest Sense

by Emily Dickinson

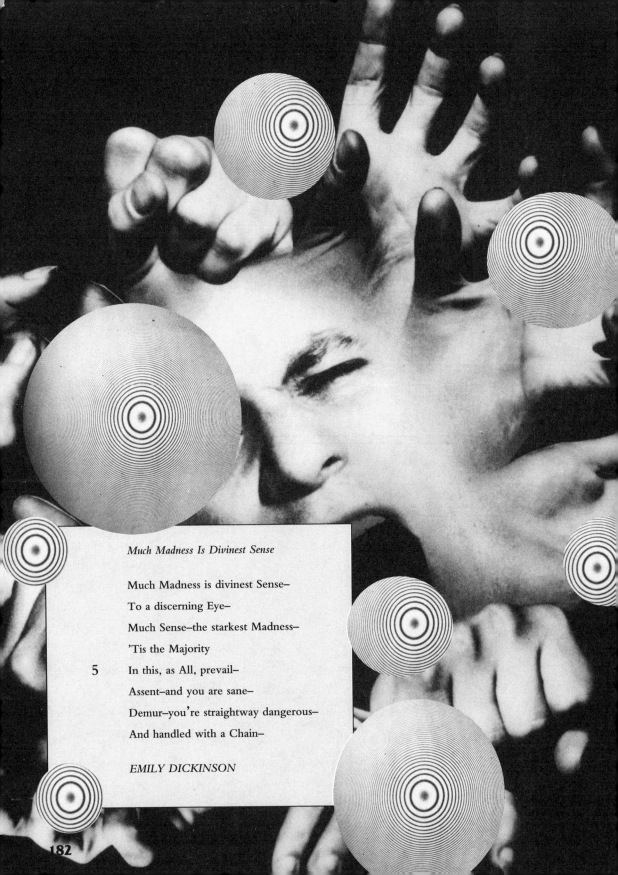

Much Madness Is Divinest Sense

Much Madness is divinest Sense—
To a discerning Eye—
Much Sense—the starkest Madness—
'Tis the Majority
5   In this, as All, prevail—
Assent—and you are sane—
Demur—you're straightway dangerous—
And handled with a Chain—

EMILY DICKINSON

Glossary

First Practice

to rupture — to break; an injury in which there is a break in the body's tissues.

What Do I Remember of the Evacuation?

"the evacuation" — To evacuate means to remove people from a place. In this case, it refers to the forced removal of Japanese-Canadians from their homes and businesses during World War II. They were taken to "internment camps" on order of the Canadian government, in order to prevent any solidarity between them and the Japanese.

to be herded — to be directed or forced to move in a certain direction, like cattle (cows)

to abandon — to leave

Gulliver of "Gulliver's Travels" — a man from a famous story, "Gulliver's Travels." He visits a land of tiny people, where he appears like a giant.

to scan — to look over

to bruise — to harm

Much Madness is Divinest Sense

divine — godly, most excellent, magnificent

to discern — to see sharply; to see the differences between

stark — complete, extreme

`tis — it is

to prevail — to win, to succeed, to dominate

to assent — to agree

sane — normal, not crazy

demur — to disagree, to object to

straightway — at once, immediately

Unit 4 Projects

I.Poetry presentation

Get into groups of three or four. Your group will be assigned one of the following poems: "First Practice," "What Do I Remember of the Evacuation?" or "Much Madness is Divinest Sense." You have four tasks:

1. Prepare a paraphrase of the literal meaning of the poem. That is, rewrite the poem's "facts" (who, what, when, where) in your own words. Use simple English.

2. Identify two ways the poet uses language in a special way to convey meaning.

    Examples: metaphor, punctuation, onomatopoeia, choice of vocabulary, symbol.

3. Prepare a statement of the poem's theme. You will read the paraphrase, analysis of language, and theme statement to the class.

4. Prepare a choral reading of the poem, to be performed for the rest of the class.

HINT FOR THE CHORAL READING:

In order to read the poem with meaning and feeling, your group should first discuss the meaning of the poem (questions l, 2, 3 above). When you read it as a group, you may have everyone read all of the lines together, or give certain people certain parts. Vary the volume, speed, and emphasis. This choral reading is a dramatic reading, and the purpose is for your group to read the poem in such a way that its tone and meaning are clear to the audience.

Your group should decide in what order to present the information from questions 1 to 3 above. One effective way is to present the choral reading at the beginning, give the explanation, and then repeat the reading.

II. Small-Group Presentation

For this project, you will be making a "semi-formal" presentation (5 to 8 minutes) about the literature of this unit and leading a discussion (5 minutes). The procedure is the same as is outlined at the end of Unit 2 ("Oral Character Analysis: Small-Group Presentation") on pages 77-78.

Possible Topics:

1. Compare and contrast two stories, two poems, or one poem and one story from this unit. Possible points of comparison and contrast are: character, narrator and speaker, conflict, tone, use of language, theme.

2. Classify the "powerless" and the "powerful" of these stories and poems. What qualities does each group share?

Prepare your notes on presentation cards (as demonstrated on pages 78-79) and make up discussion questions about your topic in order to lead a short discussion. Practice your presentation at home. You will make the presentation to a small group of three or four people.

III. Essay

Write a three- to five-page essay based on the notes of your presentation and discussion.

UNIT 5

THE USE OF FORCE

▲▲▲▲▲

Trifles

A PLAY BY SUSAN GLASPELL

Trifles

BY SUSAN GLASPELL

"It was an awful thing was done in this house that night, Mrs. Hale. Killing a man while he slept, slipping a rope around his neck that choked the life out of him."

PRE-READING

Background:

A murder mystery in one act, *Trifles* has been performed frequently in North America since its first performance in 1916. As in other detective-type stories, our job is find a "motive" for the crime in order to identify the murderer. Not only by clues discovered in the house, but by psychological "character" clues given by the neighbors, do we finally come to a satisfactory, if grim, explanation.

Warm-up Activity:

Read the following background information:

Characters:

Sheriff Peters: a middle-aged man, dressed for cold weather

County Attorney: a young man, dressed for cold weather

Mr. Hale: a middle-aged man, dressed for cold weather, one of the "witnesses"

Mrs. Peters: a slight, wiry, thin faced, nervous woman, married to the sheriff

Mrs. Hale: a large woman, normally comfortable looking, who now looks troubled

(Absent: Mr. John Wright–murdered

Mrs. Minnie Foster Wright–his wife, now in jail as a suspect for his murder)

Background:

There has been a murder. Mr. Hale and his friend "Harry," two farmers, claim to have found a strange situation at the Wright farmhouse the morning before when they dropped in to visit. Mr. Hale claims that Mrs. Wright was sitting in a rocking chair, looking "strange," and Mr. Wright was upstairs, dead in bed.

When they asked Mrs. Wright who killed him, she said she didn't know. Mr. Hale and Harry immediately called the police.

The play opens in the kitchen of John Wright's empty farmhouse. The men–Sheriff Peters, the County Attorney, and Mr. Hale–are searching for clues to help them figure out who killed John Wright. The women–Mrs. Hale and Mrs. Peters–are there to gather some clothing for Mrs. Wright, who is in jail as a suspect.

Class directions:

One half of the class will take the part of the women, and the other half, of the men. It will be easier if you work in groups of three or four. You will be predicting the plot of this play from the above information and your own imagination. You can add any details you wish to make an interesting plot.

Women: What clues might you find in the kitchen which point to the identity and the motivation of the murderer?

Men: What clues might you find upstairs and outside which point to the identity and the motivation of the murderer?

When you have finished, exchange places with someone from the other half of the class, and present your group's prediction.

If there is time, begin to read the play out loud in groups of five. Finish reading the play at home, keeping the following question in mind:

What information do we learn, little by little, about Mr. John Wright (his character) and Mrs. Minnie Foster Wright (her character and her background)?

SCENE:

The kitchen in the now abandoned farmhouse of JOHN
WRIGHT, a gloomy kitchen, and left without having been
put in order–unwashed pans under the sink, a loaf of bread
outside the bread-box, a dish-towel on the table–other signs
of incomplete work. At the rear the outer door opens and the
SHERIFF comes in followed by the COUNTY ATTORNEY
and HALE. The SHERIFF and HALE are men in middle life,
the COUNTY ATTORNEY is a young man; all are much
bundled up and go at once to the stove. They are followed by
the two women-the SHERIFF'S wife first; she is a slight wiry
woman, a thin nervous face. MRS. HALE is larger and would
ordinarily be called more comfortable looking, but she is
disturbed now and looks fearfully about as she enters. The
women have come in slowly, and stand close together near
the door.

COUNTY ATTORNEY

[Rubbing his hands.] This feels good. Come up to the fire,
ladies.

MRS. PETERS

[After taking a step forward.] I'm not–cold.

SHERIFF

[Unbuttoning his overcoat and stepping away from the
stove as if to mark the beginning of official business.] Now,
Mr. Hale, before we move things about, you explain to Mr.
Henderson just what you saw when you came here yesterday
morning.

COUNTY ATTORNEY

By the way, has anything been moved? Are things just as
you left them yesterday?

SHERIFF

[Looking about.] It's just the same. When it dropped below
zero last night I thought I'd better send Frank out this

morning to make a fire for us—no use getting pneumonia with
a big case on, but I told him not to touch anything except
the stove—and you know Frank.

COUNTY ATTORNEY

Somebody should have been left here yesterday.

SHERIFF

Oh—yesterday. When I had to send Frank to Morris Center
for that man who went crazy—I want you to know I had my
hands full yesterday. I knew you could get back from Omaha
by today and as long as I went over everything here myself—

COUNTY ATTORNEY

Well, Mr. Hale, tell just what happened when you came
here yesterday morning.

HALE

Harry and I had started to town with a load of potatoes.
We came along the road from my place and as I got here I
said, "I'm going to see if I can't get John Wright to go in
with me on a party telephone." I spoke to Wright about it
once before and he put me off, saying folks talked too much
anyway, and all he asked was peace and quiet—I guess you
know about how much he talked himself; but I thought
maybe if I went to the house and talked about it before his
wife, though I said to Harry that I didn't know as what his
wife wanted made much difference to John—

COUNTY ATTORNEY

Let's talk about that later, Mr. Hale. I do want to talk
about that, but tell now just what happened when you got to
the house.

HALE

I didn't hear or see anything; I knocked at the door, and
still it was all quiet inside. I knew they must be up, it was
past eight o'clock. So I knocked again, and I thought I heard
somebody say, "Come in." I wasn't sure, I'm not sure yet, but

I opened the door–this door [indicating the door by which the two women are still standing] and there in that rocker–[pointing to it] sat Mrs. Wright.

70 [They all look at the rocker.]

COUNTY ATTORNEY

What–was she doing?

HALE

She was rockin' back and forth. She had her apron in her
75 hand and was kind of–pleating it.

COUNTY ATTORNEY

And how did she–look?

HALE

Well, she looked queer.

80 COUNTY ATTORNEY

How do you mean–queer?

HALE

Well, as if she didn't know what she was going to do next.
And kind of done up.

85 COUNTY ATTORNEY

How did she seem to feel about your coming?

HALE

Why, I don't think she minded–one way or other. She
didn't pay much attention. I said, "How do, Mrs. Wright, it's
90 cold, ain't it?" And she said, "Is it?"–and went on kind of
pleating at her apron. Well, I was surprised; she didn't ask
me to come up to the stove, or to set down, but just sat
there, not even looking at me, so I said, "I want to see John."
And then she–laughed. I guess you would call it a laugh. I
95 thought of Harry and the team outside, so I said a little
sharp: "Can't I see John?" "No," she says, kind o' dull like.
"Ain't he home?" says I. "Yes," says she, "he's home." "Then
why can't I see him?" I asked her, out of patience. "'Cause

100 he's dead," says she. "*Dead?*" says I. She just nodded her head, not getting a bit excited, but rockin' back and forth. "Why—where is he?" says I, not knowing what to say. She just pointed upstairs—like that [himself pointing to the room above]. I got up, with the idea of going up there. I walked from there to here—then I says, "Why, what did he die of?"

105 "He died of a rope around his neck," says she, and just went on pleatin' at her apron. Well, I went out and called Harry. I thought I might—need help. We went upstairs and there he was lyin'-

   COUNTY ATTORNEY

110 I think I'd rather have you go into that upstairs, where you can point it all out. Just go on now with the rest of the story.

   HALE

   Well, my first thought was to get that rope off. It looked...[Stops, his face twitches]... but Harry, he went up to
115 him, and he said, "No, he's dead all right, and we'd better not touch anything." So we went back down stairs. She was still sitting that same way. "Has anybody been notified?" I asked. "No," says she, unconcerned. "Who did this, Mrs. Wright?" said Harry. He said it business-like—and she stopped
120 pleatin' of her apron. "I don't know," she says. "You don't *know?*" says Harry. "No," says she. "Weren't you sleepin' in the bed with him?" says Harry. "Yes," says she, "but I was on the inside." "Somebody slipped a rope round his neck and strangled him and you didn't wake up?" says Harry. "I didn't
125 wake up," she said after him. We must 'a looked as if we didn't see how that could be, for after a minute she said, "I sleep sound." Harry was going to ask her more questions but I said maybe we ought to let her tell her story first to the coroner, or the sheriff, so Harry went fast as he could to
130 Rivers' place, where there's a telephone.

   COUNTY ATTORNEY

   And what did Mrs. Wright do when she knew that you

had gone for the coroner?

HALE

135 She moved from that chair to this one over here [Pointing to a small chair in the corner] and just sat there with her hands held together and looking down. I got a feeling that I ought to make some conversation, so I said I had come in to see if John wanted to put in a telephone, and at that she

140 started to laugh, and then she stopped and looked at me-scared. [The COUNTY ATTORNEY, who has had his notebook out, makes a note.] I dunno, maybe it wasn't scared. I wouldn't like to say it was. Soon Harry got back,

145 and then Dr. Lloyd came, and you, Mr. Peters, and so I guess that's all I know that you don't.

COUNTY ATTORNEY

[Looking around.] I guess we'll go upstairs first-and then out to the barn and around there. [To the SHERIFF.] You're

150 convinced that there was nothing important here-nothing that would point to any motive.

SHERIFF

Nothing here but kitchen things.

[The COUNTY ATTORNEY, after again looking around

155 the kitchen, opens the door of a cupboard closet. He gets up on a chair and looks on a shelf. Pulls his hand away, sticky.

COUNTY ATTORNEY

Here's a nice mess.

[The women draw nearer.]

160 MRS. PETERS

[To the other woman.] Oh, her fruit; it did freeze. [To the LAWYER.] She worried about that when it turned so cold. She said the fire'd go out and her jars would break.

SHERIFF

165 Well, can you beat the women! Held for murder and

worryin' about her preserves.

COUNTY ATTORNEY

I guess before we're through she may have something more serious than preserves to worry about.

HALE

170   Well, women are used to worrying over trifles.

[The two women move a little closer together.]

COUNTY ATTORNEY

[With the gallantry of a young politician.] And yet, for all their worries, what would we do without the ladies? [The
175   women do not unbend. He goes to the sink, takes a dipperful of water from the pail and pouring it into a basin, washes his hands. Starts to wipe them on the roller-towel, turns it for a cleaner place.] Dirty towels! [Kicks his foot against the pans under the sink.] Not much of a housekeeper, would you say,
180   ladies?

MRS. HALE

[Stiffly.] There's a great deal of work to be done on a farm.

COUNTY ATTORNEY

To be sure. And yet [With a little bow to her] I know
185   there are some Dickson county farmhouses which do not have such roller towels.

[He gives it a pull to expose its full length again.]

MRS. HALE

Those towels get dirty awful quick. Men's hands aren't
190   always as clean as they might be.

COUNTY ATTORNEY

Ah, loyal to your sex, I see. But you and Mrs. Wright were neighbors. I suppose you were friends, too.

MRS. HALE

195   [Shaking her head.] I've not seen much of her of late years. I've not been in this house–it's more than a year.

COUNTY ATTORNEY

And why was that? You didn't like her?

MRS. HALE

200   I liked her all well enough. Farmers' wives have their hands full, Mr. Henderson. And then–

COUNTY ATTORNEY

Yes–?

MRS. HALE

205   [Looking about.] It never seemed a very cheerful place.

COUNTY ATTORNEY

No–it's not cheerful. I shouldn't say she had the homemaking instinct.

MRS. HALE

210   Well, I don't know as Wright had, either.

COUNTY ATTORNEY

You mean that they didn't get on very well?

MRS. HALE

No, I don't mean anything. But I don't think a place'd be
215   any cheerfuller for John Wright's being in it.

COUNTY ATTORNEY

I'd like to talk more of that a little later. I want to get the lay of things upstairs now.

[He goes to the left, where three steps lead to a stair door.]

220   SHERIFF

I suppose anything Mrs. Peters does'll be all right. She was to take in some clothes for her, you know, and a few little things. We left in such a hurry yesterday.

COUNTY ATTORNEY

225   Yes, but I would like to see what you take, Mrs. Peters, and keep an eye out for anything that might be of use to us.

MRS. PETERS

Yes, Mr. Henderson.

[The women listen to the men's steps on the stairs, then
230   look about the kitchen.]

MRS. HALE

I'd hate to have men coming into my kitchen, snooping
around and criticizing.

[She arranges the pans under sink which the LAWYER
235   had shoved out of place.]

MRS. PETERS

Of course it's no more than their duty.

MRS. HALE

Duty's all right, but I guess that deputy sheriff that came
240   out to make the fire might have got a little of this on. [Gives
the roller towel a pull.] Wish I'd thought of that sooner.
Seems mean to talk about her for not having things slicked
up when she had to come away in such a hurry.

MRS. PETERS

245   [Who has gone to a small table in the left rear corner of
the room, and lifted one end of a towel that covers a pan.]
She had bread set.

[Stands still.]

MRS. HALE

250   [Eyes fixed on a loaf of bread beside the breadbox, which
is on a low shelf at the other side of the room. Moves slowly
toward it.] She was going to put this in there. [Picks up loaf,
then abruptly drops it. In a manner of returning to familiar
things.] It's a shame about her fruit. I wonder if it's all gone.
255   [Gets up on the chair and looks.] I think there's some here
that's all right, Mrs. Peters. Yes—here; [Holding it toward the
window] this is cherries, too. [Looking again.] I declare I
believe that's the only one. [Gets down, bottle in her hand.
Goes to the sink and wipes it off on the outside.] She'll feel
260   awful bad after all her hard work in the hot weather. I

remember the afternoon I put up my cherries last summer.

[She puts the bottle on the big kitchen table, center of the room. With a sigh, is about to sit down in the rocking-chair. Before she is seated realizes what chair it is; with a slow look at it, steps back. The chair which she has touched rocks back and forth.]

MRS. PETERS

Well, I must get those things from the front room closet. [She goes to the door at the right, but after looking into the other room, steps back.] You coming with me, Mrs. Hale? You could help me carry them.

[They go in the other room; reappear, MRS. PETERS carrying a dress and skirt, MRS. HALE following with a pair of shoes.]

MRS. PETERS

My, it's cold in there.

[She puts the clothes on the big table, and hurries to the stove.]

MRS. HALE

[Examining the skirt.] Wright was close. I think maybe that's why she kept so much to herself. She didn't even belong to the Ladies Aid. I suppose she felt she couldn't do her part, and then you don't enjoy things when you feel shabby. She used to wear pretty clothes and be lively, when she was Minnie Foster, one of the town girls singing in the choir. But that–oh, that was thirty years ago. This all you was to take in?

MRS. PETERS

She said she wanted an apron. Funny thing to want, for there isn't much to get you dirty in jail, goodness knows. But I suppose just to make her feel more natural. She said they was in the top drawer in this cupboard. Yes here. And then her little shawl that always hung behind the door. [Opens stair door and looks.] Yes, here it is.

295 [Quickly shuts door leading upstairs.]

MRS. HALE

[Abruptly moving toward her.] Mrs. Peters?

MRS. PETERS

Yes, Mrs. Hale?

300 MRS. HALE

Do you think she did it?

MRS. PETERS

[In a frightened voice.] Oh, I don't know.

MRS. HALE

305 Well, I don't think she did. Asking for an apron and her
little shawl. Worrying about her fruit.

MRS. PETERS

[Starts to speak, glances up, where footsteps are heard in
the room above. In a low voice.] Mr. Peters says it looks bad

310 for her. Mr. Henderson is awful sarcastic in a speech and he'll
make fun of her sayin' she didn't wake up.

MRS. HALE

Well, I guess John Wright didn't wake when they was
slipping that rope under his neck.

315 MRS. PETERS

No, it's strange. It must have been done awful crafty and
still. They say it was such a—funny way to kill a man, rigging
it all up like that.

MRS. HALE

320 That's just what Mr. Hale said. There was a gun in the
house. He says that's what he can't understand.

MRS. PETERS

Mr. Henderson said coming out that what was needed for
the case was a motive; something to show anger, or—

325 sudden feeling.

MRS. HALE

[Who is standing by the table.] Well, I don't see any signs of anger around here. [She puts her hand on the dish towel which lies on the table, stands looking down at table, one
330 half of which is clean, the other half messy.] It's wiped to here. [Makes a move as if to finish work, then turns and looks at loaf of bread outside the breadbox. Drops towel. In that voice of coming back to familiar things.] Wonder how they are finding things upstairs. I hope she had it a little more
335 red-up up there. You know, it seems kind of *sneaking*. Locking her up in town and then coming out here and trying to get her own house to turn against her!

MRS. PETERS

But Mrs. Hale, the law is the law.

340 MRS. HALE

I s'pose 'tis. [Unbuttoning her coat.] Better loosen up your things, Mrs. Peters. You won't feel them when you go out.

[MRS. PETERS takes off her fur tippet, goes to hang it on hook at back of room, stands looking at the under part of the
345 small corner table.

MRS. PETERS

She was piecing a quilt.

[She brings the large sewing basket and they look at the bright pieces.]

350 MRS. HALE

It's log cabin pattern. Pretty, isn't it? I wonder if she was goin' to quilt it or just knot it?

[Footsteps have been heard coming down the stairs. The SHERIFF enters followed by HALE and the COUNTY
355 ATTORNEY.]

SHERIFF

They wonder if she was going to quilt it or just knot it!

[The men laugh, the women look abashed.]

COUNTY ATTORNEY

360   [Rubbing his hands over the stove.] Frank's fire didn't do much up there, did it? Well, let's go out to the barn and get that cleared up.

[The men go outside.]

MRS. HALE

365   [Resentfully.] I don't know as there's anything so strange, our takin' up our time with little things while we're waiting for them to get the evidence. [She sits down at the big table smoothing out a block with decision.] I don't see as it's anything to laugh about.

370   MRS. PETERS

[Apologetically.] Of course they've got awful important things on their minds.

[Pulls up a chair and joins MRS. HALE at the table.]

MRS. HALE

375   [Examining another block.] Mrs. Peters, look at this one. Here, this is the one she was working on, and look at the sewing! All the rest of it has been so nice and even. And look at this! It's all over the place! Why, it looks as if she didn't know what she was about!

380   [After she has said this they look at each other, then start to glance back at the door. After an instant MRS. HALE has pulled at a knot and ripped the sewing.]

MRS. PETERS

Oh, what are you doing, Mrs. Hale?

385   MRS. HALE

[Mildly.] Just pulling out a stitch or two that's not sewed very good. [Threading a needle.] Bad sewing always made me fidgety.

MRS. PETERS

390 [Nervously.] I don't think we ought to touch things.

MRS. HALE

I'll just finish up this end. [Suddenly stopping and leaning forward.] Mrs. Peters?

MRS. PETERS

395 Yes, Mrs. Hale?

MRS. HALE

What do you suppose she was so nervous about?

MRS. PETERS

Oh-I don't know. I don't know as she was nervous. I
400 sometimes sew awful queer when I'm just tired. [MRS.
HALE starts to say something, looks at MRS. PETERS, then
goes on sewing.] Well I must get these things wrapped up.
They may be through sooner than we think. [Putting apron
and other things together.] I wonder where I can find a piece
of paper, and string.

405 MRS. HALE

In that cupboard, maybe.

MRS. PETERS

[Looking in cupboard.] Why, here's a bird-cage. [Holds it
up.] Did she have a bird, Mrs. Hale?

410 MRS. HALE

Why, I don't know whether she did or not-I've not been
here for so long. There was a man around last year selling
canaries cheap, but I don't know as she took one; maybe she
did. She used to sing real pretty herself.

415 MRS. PETERS

[Glancing around.] Seems funny to think of a bird here.
But she must have had one, or why would she have a cage? I
wonder what happened to it.

MRS. HALE

420   I s'pose maybe the cat got it.

MRS. PETERS

No, she didn't have a cat. She's got that feeling some
people have about cats—being afraid of them. My cat got in
her room and she was real upset and asked me to take it out.

425   MRS. HALE

My sister Bessie was like that. Queer, ain't it?

MRS. PETERS

[Examining the cage.] Why, look at this door. It's broke.
One hinge is pulled apart.

430   MRS. HALE

[Looking too.] Looks as if someone must have been rough
with it.

MRS. PETERS

Why, yes.

435   [She brings the cage forward and puts it on the table.]

MRS. HALE

I wish if they're going to find any evidence they'd be about
it. I don't like this place.

MRS. PETERS

440   But I'm awful glad you came with me, Mrs. Hale. It would
be lonesome for me sitting here alone.

MRS. HALE

It would, wouldn't it? [Dropping her sewing.] But I tell
you what I do wish, Mrs. Peters. I wish I had come over

445   sometimes when she was here. I–[Looking around the
room]–wish I had.

MRS. PETERS

But of course you were awful busy, Mrs. Hale-your house
and your children.

450   MRS. HALE

I could've come. I stayed away because it weren't cheerful–
and that's why I ought to have come. I–I've never liked this
place. Maybe because it's down in a hollow and you don't see
the road. I dunno what it is, but it's a lonesome place and
always was. I wish I had come over to see Minnie Foster
sometimes. I can see now–

[Shakes her head.]

MRS. PETERS

Well, you mustn't reproach yourself, Mrs. Hale. Somehow
we just don't see how it is with other folks until–something
comes up.

MRS. HALE

Not having children makes less work–but it makes a quiet
house, and Wright out to work all day, and no company
when he did come in. Did you know John Wright, Mrs.
Peters?

MRS. PETERS

Not to know him; I've seen him in town. They say he was
a good man.

MRS. HALE

Yes–good; he didn't drink, and kept his word as well as
most, I guess, and paid his debts. But he was a hard man,
Mrs. Peters. Just to pass the time of day with him–[Shivers.]
Like a raw wind that gets to the bone. [Pauses, her eye falling
on the cage.] I should think she would 'a wanted a bird. But
what do you suppose went with it?

MRS. PETERS

I don't know, unless it got sick and died.

[She reaches over and swings the broken door, swings it
again, both women watch it.]

MRS. HALE

You weren't raised round here, were you? [MRS. PETERS

shakes her head.] You didn't know—her?

MRS. PETERS

485   Not till they brought her yesterday.

MRS. HALE

She—come to think of it, she was kind of like a bird herself—real sweet and pretty, but kind of timid and—fluttery. How—she—did—change. [Silence; then as if struck by a happy
490   thought and relieved to get back to every day things.] Tell you what, Mrs. Peters, why don't you take the quilt in with you? It might take up her mind.

MRS. PETERS

Why, I think that's a real nice idea, Mrs. Hale. There
495   couldn't possibly be any objection to it, could there? Now, just what would I take? I wonder if her patches are in here— and her things.

[They look in the sewing basket.]

MRS. HALE

500   Here's some red. I expect this has got sewing things in it. [Brings out a fancy box.] What a pretty box. Looks like something somebody would give you. Maybe her scissors are in here. [Opens box. Suddenly puts her hand to her nose.] Why—[MRS. PETERS bends nearer, then turns her face
505   away.] There's something wrapped up in this piece of silk.

MRS. PETERS

Why, this isn't her scissors.

MRS. HALE

[Lifting the silk.] Oh, Mrs. Peters—it's—

510   [MRS. PETERS bends closer.]

MRS. PETERS

It's the bird.

MRS. HALE

[Jumping up.] But, Mrs. Peters—look at it! Its neck! Look at

515   its neck! It's all–other side to.

        MRS. PETERS

        Somebody–wrung–its–neck.

        [Their eyes meet. A look of growing comprehension, of
        horror. Steps are heard outside. MRS. HALE slips box under
520   quilt pieces, and sinks into her chair.]

        Enter SHERIFF and COUNTY ATTORNEY. MRS.
        PETERS rises.

        COUNTY ATTORNEY

        [As one turning from serious things to little pleasantries.]
525   Well, ladies have you decided whether she was going to quilt
        it or knot it?

        MRS. PETERS

        We think she was going to–knot it.

        COUNTY ATTORNEY

530   Well, that's interesting, I'm sure. [Seeing the birdcage.] Has
        the bird flown?

        MRS. HALE

        [Putting more quilt pieces over the box.] We think the–cat
        got it.

535   COUNTY ATTORNEY

        [Preoccupied.] Is there a cat?

        [MRS. HALE glances in a quick covert way at MRS.
        PETERS.

        MRS. PETERS

540   Well, not now. They're superstitious, you know. They
        leave.

        COUNTY ATTORNEY

        [To SHERIFF PETERS, continuing an interrupted
        conversation.] No sign at all of anyone having come from the
545   outside. Their own rope. Now let's go up again and go over
        it piece by piece. [They start upstairs.] It would have to have

been someone who knew just the—]

[MRS. PETERS sits down. The two women sit there not looking at one another, but as if peering into something and at the same time holding back. When they talk now it is in the manner of feeling their way over strange ground, as if afraid of what they are saying, but as if they can not help saying it.]

MRS. HALE

She liked the bird. She was going to bury it in that pretty box.

MRS. PETERS

[In a whisper.] When I was a girl—my kitten—there was a boy took a hatchet, and before my eyes—and before I could get there—[Covers her face an instant.] If they hadn't held me back I would have—[Catches herself, looks upstairs where steps are heard, falters weakly]—hurt him.

MRS. HALE

[With a slow look around her.] I wonder how it would seem never to have had any children around. [Pause.] No, Wright wouldn't like the bird—a thing that sang. She used to sing. He killed that, too.

MRS. PETERS

[Moving uneasily.] We don't know who killed the bird.

MRS. HALE

I knew John Wright.

MRS. PETERS

It was an awful thing was done in this house that night, Mrs. Hale. Killing a man while he slept, slipping a rope around his neck that choked the life out of him.

MRS. HALE

His neck. Choked the life out of him.

[Her hand goes out and rests on the bird-cage.]

MRS. PETERS

580   [With rising voice.] We don't know who killed him. We don't *know*.

MRS. HALE

[Her own feeling not interrupted.] If there'd been years and years of nothing, then a bird to sing to you, it would be
585   awful–still, after the bird was still.

MRS. PETERS

[Something within her speaking.] I know what stillness is. When we homesteaded in Dakota, and my first baby died– after he was two years old, and me with no other then–

590   **MRS. HALE**

[Moving.] How soon do you suppose they'll be through, looking for the evidence?

MRS. PETERS

I know what stillness is. [Pulling herself back.] The law has
595   got to punish crime, Mrs. Hale.

MRS. HALE

[Not as if answering that.] I wish you'd seen Minnie Foster when she wore a white dress with blue ribbons and stood up there in the choir and sang. [A look around the room.] Oh, I
600   *wish* I'd come over here once in a while! That was a crime! That was a crime! Who's going to punish that?

MRS. PETERS

[Looking upstairs.] We mustn't–take on.

MRS. HALE

605   I might have known she needed help! I know how things can be–for women. I tell you, it's queer, Mrs. Peters. We live close together and we live far apart. We all go through the same things–it's all just a different kind of the same thing. [Brushes her eyes, noticing the bottle of fruit, reaches out for
610   it.] If I was you I wouldn't tell her her fruit was gone. Tell

her it *ain't*. Tell her it's all right. Take this in to prove it to her. She—she may never know whether it was broke or not.

MRS. PETERS

615 [Takes the bottle, looks about for something to wrap it in; takes petticoat from the clothes brought from the other room, very nervously begins winding this around the bottle. In a false voice.] My, it's a good thing the men couldn't hear us. Wouldn't they just laugh! Getting all stirred up over a little thing like a—dead canary. As if that could have anything to do
620 with—with—wouldn't they *laugh!*

[The men are heard coming down stairs.]

MRS. HALE

[Under her breath.] Maybe they would—maybe they wouldn't.

625 COUNTY ATTORNEY

No, Peters, it's all perfectly clear except a reason for doing it. But you know juries when it comes to women. If there was some definite thing. Something to show—something to make a story about—a thing that would connect up with this
630 strange way of doing it—

[The women's eyes meet for an instant. Enter HALE from outer door.]

HALE

Well, I've got the team around. Pretty cold out there.

635 COUNTY ATTORNEY

I'm going to stay here a while by myself. [To the SHERIFF.] You can send Frank out for me, can't you? I want to go over everything. I'm not satisfied that we can't do better.

640 SHERIFF

Do you want to see what Mrs. Peters is going to take in?

[The LAWYER goes to the table, picks up the apron, laughs.]

COUNTY ATTORNEY

645 Oh, I guess they're not very dangerous things the ladies have picked out. [Moves a few things about, disturbing the quilt pieces which cover the box. Steps back.] No, Mrs. Peters doesn't need supervising. For that matter, a sheriff's wife is married to the law. Ever think of it that way, Mrs.
650 Peters?

MRS. PETERS

Not–just that way.

SHERIFF

[Chuckling.] Married to the law. [Moves toward the other
655 room.] I just want you to come in here a minute, George. We ought to take a look at these windows.

COUNTY ATTORNEY

[Scoffingly.] Oh, windows!

SHERIFF

660 We'll be right out, Mr. Hale. [HALE goes outside. The SHERIFF follows the COUNTY ATTORNEY into the other room. Then MRS. HALE rises, hands tight together, looking intensely at MRS. PETERS, whose eyes make a slow turn, finally meeting MRS. HALE'S. A moment MRS. HALE
665 holds her, then her own eyes point the way to where the box is concealed. Suddenly MRS. PETERS throws back quilt pieces and tries to put the box in the bag she is wearing. It is too big. She opens box, starts to take bird out, cannot touch it, goes to pieces, stands there helpless. Sound of knob
670 turning in the other room. MRS. HALE snatches the box and puts it in the pocket of her big coat. Enter COUNTY ATTORNEY and SHERIFF.]

COUNTY ATTORNEY

[Facetiously.] Well, Henry, at least we found out that she
675   was not going to quilt it. She was going to—what is it you call
it, ladies?

MRS. HALE

[Her hand against her pocket.] We call it—knot it, Mr.
Henderson.

680   (CURTAIN)

ACT IT OUT

1. In pairs, read out loud the parts of Mr. Hale and the County Attorney, from line 62 to line 146. How would you describe the reaction of Mrs. Wright, as described by Hale?

2. Next, re-create (and write down) the dialogue between Mr. Hale and Mrs. Wright, based on the testimony of Mr. Hale (lines 62-146). The situation is that described by Mr. Hale, when he first arrives at the farmhouse and finds Mrs. Wright in the rocking chair. When you have finished writing the dialogue, one of you should take the role of Mr. Hale and the other of Mrs. Wright, and you should act out the scene. A few pairs may perform for the class.

Example:

(Mrs. Wright is sitting in the rocker, pleating her apron with her hand, looking rather confused)

MR HALE
"Hello, Mrs. Wright. It's cold, isn't it?"

MRS. WRIGHT
"Is it?" (continues pleating her apron)

Comprehension

Complete the following plot graph. What are the clues found by the women, but not by the men? Why don't the women tell the men about the clues? What conflicts drive the rising action?

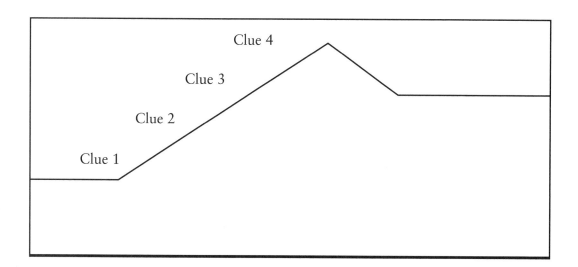

Clue 4

Clue 3

Clue 2

Clue 1

In groups of three, read the dialogue between Mrs. Hale, Mrs. Peters, and the County Attorney, from "Here's some red. . ." to "Well, that's interesting, I'm sure." (lines 500-530) You must use a lot of emotional expression to act out this scene. Imagine the feelings of the characters. What tone of voice does the County Attorney use when he enters?

Comprehension and Interpretation

To complete this character chart, you need to either think of an adjective and/or a phrase that describes the character, or find evidence (quotations) from the play text which supports the description. Fill in the missing information.

Mrs. Minnie Foster Wright

Character	Evidence from the text
Lonely	silent husband no telephone no children "what his wife wanted didn't make much difference to John" (57)
	"it never seemed a very cheerful place." (205)
hardworking	
	"Mr. Wright was close. I think maybe that's why she kept so much to herself." (280)
had been happy and pretty when young	
probably about 50 years old	
creative	

Mr. John Wright

Character	Evidence from the text
silent	"people talk too much" (52) no telephone
	"I don't think a place would be any cheerfuller for John Wright's being in it." (215)
stingy	
	"He was a good man; he didn't drink, and he kept his word and paid his debts." (471)
harsh, unkind	

Response Check

What do you think about Mrs. Wright? Do you sympathize with her? Do you know any married couple like the Wrights?

Interpretation

1. Mrs. Hale compares Mrs. Minnie Foster Wright to the bird (line 486). Why? Who else might be compared to the bird?

2. A mystery or detective story often has two plot developments–the search for clues, and the "real story," which usually happened before the play or novel begins, and which the clues represent or point to. You have diagrammed the discovery of clues by the women; now complete the plot graph below to represent the "real story":

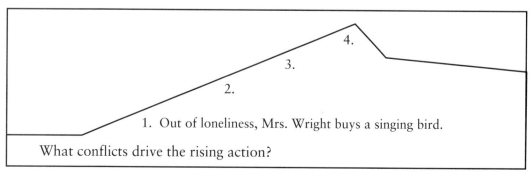

4.

3.

2.

1. Out of loneliness, Mrs. Wright buys a singing bird.

What conflicts drive the rising action?

Act It Out

With a partner, create the scene between Mr. and Mrs. Wright in which Mr. Wright decides to kill the bird. After you have written the dialogue, practice acting it out. Some of you may be asked to perform your dialogues for the class.

Interpretation

We have examined the use of irony in many of the stories in this textbook. Remember, irony is the use of words to express the *opposite* of their literal or usual meaning. Irony results when there is a difference between our expectations and what actually happens. In drama, irony often occurs when the audience knows information which the characters in the play don't know.

This play is full of ironies. Explain the irony of the following statements. Can you find any others in the play?

a. Nothing here but kitchen things. (line 152)

b. I wish if they're going to find any evidence, they would be about it. (line 436)

c. We think she was going to. . . knot it. (line 527)

d. His neck. Choked the life out of him. (line 576)

e. the title–Trifles

Evaluation: Discussion or Response Journal

MRS. PETERS
I know what stillness is. (Pulling herself back.) The law has got to punish crime,
Mrs. Hale.

MRS. HALE

(Not as if answering that.) I wish you'd seen Minnie Foster when she wore a white dress
with blue ribbons and stood up there in the choir and sang. (A look around the room.) Oh
I wish I'd come over here once in a while! That was a crime! That was a crime! Who's
going to punish that?

What does Mrs. Hale mean by "that" in "That was a crime!"? Do you agree? Make a list
of the "crimes" of the play, and rank them according to how serious they are. Do you
blame Mrs. Minnie Foster Wright for what she did? Do you think the women should tell
the police about the clues they discovered? Would you?

How does this conversation relate to a theme in the play? What other themes can you
think of?

Conversation Round

The situation: Imagine Mrs. Hale visits Mrs. Wright in jail. What kind of conversation do
they have?

Directions:

1. The class should sit in a circle, with a pen and paper in hand.

2. First, each student writes the first utterance, imagining that they are Mrs. Hale.

3. Everyone passes their paper to their right-hand neighbor.

4. Everyone reads the utterance, and then imagining that they are Mrs. Wright, writes a
   reply to it on the paper.

5. Everyone passes the paper back to their left-hand neighbor (who wrote the original
   utterance).

6. Everyone is now Mrs. Hale again, and replies to Mrs. Wright's utterance.

7. Continue until the time is up.

8. Everyone should then read out loud their complete dialogue with their right-hand
   neighbor, and then with their left-hand neighbor.

Unit Five Projects

I. **TV panel**

Each group must prepare and present a short report on the events of the play, as if they were participating in a special TV news report.

In each group you will need: an interviewer, Sheriff Peters, Mr. Hale, Mrs. Hale, Mrs. Peters, Mrs. Minnie Foster Wright.

Each group prepares scripts for a TV interview. The special reports are presented in front of the class.

II. **Essay**

In a three- to five-page essay, discuss the conflicts of the play, and the patterns of power and powerlessness which result. In the end, who is more powerful, the men or the women?